A Passage to Neuroscience of Leadership

A Passage to Neuroscience of Leadership

Fakir Mohan Sahoo

Ph.D. (Queen's, Canada)
Formerly Professor & Head of the Dept. of Psychology
Centre of Advanced Study in Psychology
Utkal University, Bhubaneswar, India

At present Visiting Professor
XIM University, Bhubaneswar, India

BLACK EAGLE BOOKS
DUBLIN, USA | BHUBANESWAR, INDIA

BLACK EAGLE BOOKS

USA address:
7464 Wisdom Lane
Dublin, OH 43016

India address:
E/312, Trident Galaxy, Kalinga Nagar,
Bhubaneswar-751003, Odisha, India

E-mail: info@blackeaglebooks.org
Website: www.blackeaglebooks.org

First International Edition Published by
BLACK EAGLE BOOKS, 2022

A PASSAGE TO NEUROSCIENCE OF LEADERSHIP
by **Fakir Mohan Sahoo**

Cover & Interior Design: Ezy's Publication

ISBN- 978-1-64560-343-6 (Paperback)
Library of Congress Control Number: 2023930858

Printed in the United States of America

To
Profs. R.N. Kanungo, J.P. Das and **A.P. Purohit**
–a leadingpsychologists of Odisha who have navigated the flagship of Psychology beyond national borders.

- FMS

CONTENTS

Preface

Neuroscience has become a buzz-word in contempory lives. The neuroscience research came in a big way when Roger Sperry received Noble Prize for his split-brain research. Since mid-eighties, Neuroscience has expanded new possibilities, highlighted unexplored areas of knowledge and has provided connectivity amongst many fields. New topics have been identified, novel concerns have been expressed and many solutions have been generated.

In the context of leadership research, this New Look Approach has opened new frontiers of knowledge. A number of issues in leadership that remained unexplainable in the past are now examined through neuroscientific lenses. The initial explorations have generated optimistic outcomes. Since neuroscientific investigation is relatively a new entry into our leadership arena, the furthering of such efforts is likely to yield promising dividends.

23 November 2022   **F. M. Sahoo**

Chapter 1

Introduction

Neuroscience is changing our understanding of how the human brain works and how and why people behave the way they do. Properly understood, many of these insights could lead to profound changes in the way business world operates.

What makes a great leader? This profoundly important question has been on the minds of scientists, philosophers, professionals and even ordinary citizens around the globe for centuries. The search for the answer has followed many paths, adopted many strategies and experimented many propositions. Yet, the result was far from being satisfactory. It appeared that a *paradigm crisis* was to be resolved.

The advent of neuroscience signals the *paradigm shift*. In this approach, the focus was not on systems or the external world, but on the brain, the internal world. The brain is highly resilient. It is this phenomenal capacity of the brain to change that brings leadership to the forefront of creating better organization and a better future for all.

It is asserted that leadership is based on several pillars of strength. The first pillar is the *thinking process*. It is the longest pillar because leaders are supposed to carry out analytical thinking, make judicious decisions, express opinions and articulate the judgments to relevant populations. The process of planning and decision making is a regular and essential element of leadership process.

The second pillar reflects the emotional life of our brain. Humans encounter difficulty in understanding and expressing their emotions. This creates a formidable challenge for the leader. How emotions are dimensionalized and how are they sublimated constitute important learning parameters. The study of emotional brain and its management provide very important learning inputs for the leader. The broadening and building of positive emotions helps while negative emotions drain human capacity. The sublimation of negative emotion strengthens leadership potential. The coaching process that involves the channelization of emotional energy through supportive brain activity is a helpful lever that presses the success-botton.

The third pillar involves the *brain automations*. Many automated responses and protocols of our brain (that are beyond our conscious controls) are rooted in deeper brain structures. It is imperative that leaders understand and use these automations to their advantages. Priming, the process by which leaders can nudge their brain and the brain of others towards a specific decision, should be applied. Through priming, leaders can improve productivity, creativity and social connectivity. Recent studies indicate that changing habits and creating new habits is not difficult. The principle of automation could be used to eliminate negative habits and form positive habits.

The fourth pillar involves the social skills of the leader. Utilizing brains capacity for social connectivity, this objective can be given a tangible reality. Relations are built and nurtured through communications. In communication, we need to use three main functions of the brain: think, feel and do. To get maximum results both for individual and collective brains, leaders need to use the principle of persuasions, specific words or phrases that can fast-track their influence to others, and compassionate conversations and they key stimuli of getting brain's attention.

The **brain-adaptive leaders (BAL Approach)** is not only useful for understanding and harnessing primary objectives such as thinking, sublimating negative emotions, leveraging social relations and the use of priming, it is also instrumental for cultivating and strengthening special attributes.

It is important to recognize that BAL Approach is helpful for evolving a new science of leadership. Effective leaders are less stressed and studies of neuroscience not only provide scientific knowledge for understanding stress, it is useful for transforming negative energy into positive forms. The possibility that leaders can have more testosterone and less cortisol can be achieved through neuroscientific intervention. Similarly, the building of self-efficacy (self-confidence) becomes a distinct possibility through the use of BAL approach.

It has been well-accepted in brain science that prefrontal cortex (PFC) plays a vital role in planning, decision-making, emotional regulation and multi-tasking. How can we further develop higher executive functions of the prefrontal cortex? There are behavioural routes for such positive growth and maintenance.

Finally, it is asserted that leaders need to be competent and knowledgeable. Neuroscience is a vast source of inputs that empower leaders in the direction of effectiveness.

Leaders are like experts. In order to be successful, they need to be competent, to have sufficient knowledge in order to act in ways which are more likely to benefit than harm the organization they lead, more likely to lead in success than failure. Competence is taken as a domain expertise in the specific area of business, industry or market in which their organization operates.

The neuroscience offers us an optimistic outlook that the PFC can be developed and its capacity enhanced through focused attention and practice. This is a good news for the organization and leaders, because it means that leadership qualities and capabilities can be learned and improved through experience together with training and development.

Meaning, values and ethics can also be developed and furthered by enriched experience. The lessons from neuroscience present such humanistic possibility. It is true that the collective wisdom stored in our brains can pave the way for better leadership.

Chapter 2

Landmarks in Brain Research

E motions have served adaptive functions throughout human history. Emotional processes that facilitate inter individual bands (participation in group living) have selective advantage. The formation of such bonds is pleasurable for primates. They are easy to learn and hard to forget.

The emotion of interest plays a vital role in the development of skill and competencies. The threshold of one's interest is crucial to adaptation and effective functioning. This emotion guarantees response to complexity, novelty, and change. Since human beings are complex and ever changing, interest facilitates the formation and maintenance of social relationships.

Joy complements interest in guaranteeing that human beings will be social creature. A smile of joy on the human face is the most general and effective social stimulus that exists. The reciprocal smiling of mother and infant fosters attachment and the development of a strong interpersonal tie that facilitates the infant's survival and healthy development. The joy and laughter preclude the strain of negative emotions and enhance infant-environment interaction.

Surprise clears the neural pathways of other messages and prepares the individual to deal effectively with a new or sudden event and the consequences of such events. From an evolutionary standpoint surprise can be seen as the emotion that functions to change the organism's motivational set. Failure to make such a change in the face of sudden dangers could prove fatal.

The emotion of distress tells the individual that all is not well. It provides the motivation to address the problem and alleviate the distress. Distress also serves as the basis for *empathy* and altruism. It enables people to feel with the other individual who suffers. This empathetic distress motivates the individual to work towards the alleviation of suffering of others.

Anger is one of the emergency emotions. Anger mobilizes energy and renders the individual capable of defending self with great vigour and strength. It was very useful in the early history of the human species. While this function of anger become less needed with the rise of civilization, appropriately expressed anger may still be justifiable and adaptive.

During the course of evolution, disgust probably helped prevent organisms from eating spoiled food and drinking polluted water and motivated them to maintain sanitary conditions. Similarly, *contempt* may have emerged as a vehicle for preparing a group to face an adversary.

The principal function of fear in evolution is to motivate the individual to escape from danger and to mobilize necessary energy to accomplish this. Fear also serves as a force for social cohesion and collective action when the group or community is threatened.

In evolutionary terms, *shame* probably developed from a need for social norms, common patterns of socialization, and group cohesiveness. If a child's speech or manner or social behaviour does not conform with that of society, he or she may be "shamed" or subjected to contempt that leads to shame. *Guilt* and the motive to avoid guilt heighten one's sense of responsibility and moral obligation. Guilt is built-in monitor of the rules of fair play and provides the structure for social order.

The role of emotion in human functioning has been further clarified by certain biopsychological investigations of emotion. There are a number of landmarks in this context.

The Mind-Blowing Case of Gage

In 1848, Phineas Gage, a 25-year-old construction foreman for the Burlington Railroad, was the victim of a tragic accident. In order to lay new tracks, the terrain has to be leveled and Gage was in charge of blasting. On the fateful day, the gunpowder exploded prematurely. Although Gage survived the accident, but he survived it a changed man. Before the accident, Gage had been a responsible, intelligent, social, well-adapted person. Once recovered, he appeared to be as able-bodied as before, but his personality and emotional life had totally changed. Gage became irreverent and impulsive; his abundant profanity offended many. He became unpredicatable and undependable. He lost his job and was never again able to hold a responsible position. After his death, neurologist John Harlow was granted permission to study Gage's skull. In 1994, Damasia and her colleagues brought the power of computerized reconstruction to hear Gage's classic case. They begun by taking an X-ray of the skull and measuring it precisely. From these measurements, they reconstructed the accident and determined the likely region of Gage's brain damage. It was apparent that the damage to Gage's brain affected both *medical prefrontal* lobes, which are involved in planning and emotion.

Drawing on the case analysis of Gage and a few others, it can be suggested that vital functions such as memory, planning and decision-making are localized in the frontal lobe (portion just behind the forehead). **The involvement** of the frontal brain in planning and emotion is a seminal idea.

Darwin's Contribution

In 1872, Darwin's book *The Expression of Emotions in Man and Animals* is a major event. In it, Darwin argued that particular emotional expressions, such as human facial expressions, tend to accompany the same emotional status in all members of a species.

Darwin believed that *expressions of emotions are products of evolution*. His theory contained three main ideas: (1) Expressions of emotions evolve from behaviours that indicate what an organism is likely to do next: (2) if the signals provided by such behaviour benefit the organism, the signals would evolve; and (3) opposite messages are often signaled by opposite movements and postures. Darwin explained dog's aggressive postures and submissive postures with these ideas.

Bodily Changes and Emotion

Generally, we believe that we first experience emotion; this experience leads to expression of emotion. However, the first physiological theory of emotion (James & Lange, 1884) stated it otherwise. It posited that emotional experience follows emotional expression. For example, we first see a snake and start running. As we ran, we experience the emotion of fear. If we donot run and hit the snake with a stick, it would evoke emotion of aggression instead of emotion of fear. According to the James-Lange principle, emotional experience depends entirely on feedback from autonomic and somatic nervous system activity.

Later this view was changed. Cannon and Bard (1915) proposed that brain plays the major role in interpreting emotional stimuli. Hence emotional experience and emotional expressions occur simultaneously. However, both of these views (James-Lange and Canon-Bard) are part of history. Now it is believed that three principal components are involved in an emotional response. These are the perception of the emotion-inducing stimulus, the autonomic and bodily responses, and the experience of emotion.

Comparison of James-Lange versus Cannon-Bard Theories

The comparison between James-Lange and Cannon-Bard Theories of Emotion can be presented schematically.

Common-Sense View

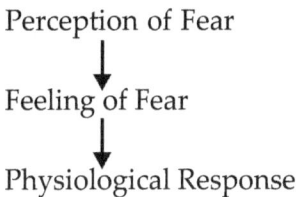

Perception of Fear
↓
Feeling of Fear
↓
Physiological Response

James-Lange View

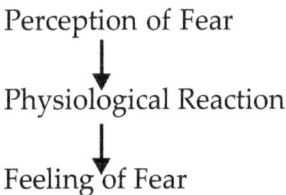

Perception of Fear
↓
Physiological Reaction
↓
Feeling of Fear

Cannon-Bard View

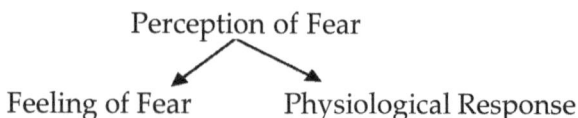

Perception of Fear

Feeling of Fear   Physiological Response

Modern Biopsychological View

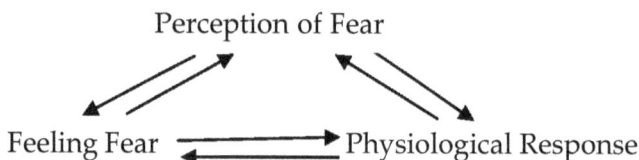

Perception of Fear

Feeling Fear ⟶ Physiological Response

The James-Lange and Cannon-Bard theories make different predictions about the role of feedback from autonomic and somatic nervous systems in emotional experience. According to James-Lange theory, emotional experience depends entirely on feedback from autonomic and somatic nervous system activities. According to the Cannon-Bard theory, emotional experience is independent of such feedback. Both extreme positions have proved to be incorrect. On the other hand, it seems that the autonomic and somatic feedback is not necessary for the experience of emotion. Human patients whose autonomic and somatic feedback has been largely eliminated by a broken neck are capable of a full range of emotional experiences. On the other hand, there have been numerous reports that autonomic and somatic responses to emotional stimuli can influence emotional experience.

Failure to find unqualified support for either the James-Lange or the Cannon-Bard theory led to a third view. According to this third view each of the three factors in emotional experience   the perception of the emotion-inducing stimuli, the autonomic and somatic responses to the stimulus, and the experience of emotion   influence the other two.

Role of Hypothalamus

In the late 1920s, Bard discovered that decorticate cats cats whose cortex has been removed   respond aggressively to the slightest provocation. After a light touch, they expose their teeth. The aggressive responses of decorticate cats are abnormal in two respects. They are not appropriate and they are not directed at particular targets. Bard referred to the exaggerated, poorly directed aggressive response of decorticate animals as sham rage.

Sham rage can be elicited in decorticate cats whose cerebral hemisphere have been removed, but not in cats whose hypothalamus has been removed. Bard concluded that the hypothalamus is critical for the expression of aggressive responses, though the function of the cortex is to inhibit and direct these responses.

In 1937, Papez (pronounced as "Payps") proposed that emotional expression is controlled by several interconnected neural structures (limbic structures). The limbic system is a collect of nuclei and tracts that borders *thalamus*. Papez proposed that emotion states are expressed through the action of limbic structures on the hypothalamus and they are experienced through the action of the limbic structures on the cortex.

Emotional Specificity of the ANS

The James-Lange and Cannon-Bard theories differ in their views of emotional specificity of the ANS. The James-Lange theory says that different emotional stimuli induce different patterns of ANS activity and that these different patterns produce different emotional experiences. In contrast, the Cannon-Bard theory claims that all emotional stimuli produce the same general pattern of sympathetic action pattern, which prepares the organism for action (i.e., increased heart rate, increased blood pressure, pupil dilchan, increased flow of blood to the muscles, increased respiration, and increased released of epinephrine and norepinephrine from the adrenal medulla).

The experimental evidence suggests that the specificity of ANS reactions lies somewhere between the extremes of total specificity and total generality. There is ample evidence that not all emotions are associated with the same pattern of ANS activity. There is also insufficient evidence to make a strong case for the view that each emotion is characterized by a different pattern of ANS activity.

Limbic System and Amygdala

In 1973, it was found that emotional expression if controlled by several interconnected neural structure called *limbic system.* it is a collection of nuclei and tracts that borders the thalamus (limbic means "border").

More specifically a specific part of limbic system, amygdala, plays a critical role in emotion. In 1939, Kluver and Bucy found a striking *syndrome* (Pattern of behaviour) in monkeys that had their amygdala removed. The syndrome known as *Kluver-Bucy syndrome* includes the following behaviour: the consumption almost anything that is edible, increased sexual activity often directed at inappropriate objects, a tendency to repeatedly investigate familiar objects and a lack of fear. **Kluver-Bucy syndrome** appears to result from amygdala damage. It is observed in several species.

A human case of Kluver-Bucy syndrome was

demonstrated in tragic way. A human patient with a brain infection exhibited a flat affect. Although originally restless, he ultimately became placid. He spent much time gazing at the television, but never learned to turn it on, when the set was off. He tended to watch reflections of others in the room on the glass screen. He smiled inappropriately and mimicked the gestures and actions of other. Once initiating an imitative series, he would perseverate copying all movements made by another for extended period of time... He engaged in oral exploration of all objects within his grasp. He appeared unable to gain information by tactile or visual means. All objects he could lift were placed on his mouth and sucked or chewed.

Although heterosexual prior to his illness, he was observed in hospital to make advances towards other male patients. He never made advances towards women. Later it was discovered the symptoms appeared to result from amygdala damage.

Exhibit: Five Landmarks

Date	Event	Implications
1848	Case of Phineas Gage	Important role of frontal lobe (brain portion behind forehead) in planning and emotion
1872	Darwin's observation	Evolutionary role of emotions (Emotions that help in adaptation)
About 1900	James-Lange & Canon-Bard Principle	Complementary role of brain autonomic Principle nervous system and bodily changes in emotion
1937	Limbic system	A collection of interconnected nuclei and tracts that borders the thalamus. It has seminal role in emotion
1939	Discovery of Kluver-Bucy syndrome	A structure of the medial temporal lobe of the brain that plays role in the memory for the emotional significance of experience. Damage to amygdala produces Kluver-Bucy Syndrome a severe disorder in emotional behaviour.

Chapter 3

Methods of Studying Brain Functions

Prior to the early 1970s, biopsychological research was impeded by the inability to obtain images of human brain. Conventional X-ray photography was of no use. For an X-ray photograph to be taken, an X-ray beam is passed through an object and then onto a photographic plate. Each of the molecules through which the beam passes absorb some of the radiation; thus, only the unabsorbed portions of the beam reach the photographic plate. X-ray photography is therefore effective in characterizing internal structures that differ substantially from their surroundings in the degree in which they absorb X-rays (For example, a revolver in a suitcase full of clothes or a bone in flesh). Since the overlapping structures of the brain differ only slightly to absorb X-rays differentially little information about brain structure is revealed.

Contrast X-Rays

Contrast X-ray techniques involve injecting into one compartment of the body a substance that absorbs X rays either less or more than the surrounding tissue. The injected substance then heightens the contrast between the compartment and the surrounding tissue during X-ray photography.

The contrast X-ray technique, **cerebral angiography**, uses the infusion of a radio-opaque dye into a cerebral artery to visualize the cerebral circulating system during X-ray photography. Cerebral angiograms are most useful for locating vascular damage, but the displacement of blood vessels from their normal positions also can indicate the location of a tumor.

X-Ray Computed Tomography

In the early 1970s, the study of the living human brain was revolutionized by the introduction of Computed tomography (CT). **Computed Tomography (CT)** is a computer assisted X-ray procedure that can be used to visualize the brain and other internal structures of the living body. During cerebral computed tomography, neurological client lies with his or her head positioned in the centre of a large cylinder. On one side of the cylinder is an X-ray tube that projects a X-ray beam through the head to an X-ray detector mounted on the other side. The X-ray tube and detector automatically rotate around the head of the target person at one level of the beam, taking many individual X-ray photographs as they rotate. The meager information in each X-ray photograph is combined by a computer to generate a CT scan of one horizontal section of the brain. Then, the X-ray tube and the detector are moved along the axis of the target's body to another level of the brain and the process is repeated. Scans of eight or nine horizontal brain sections are typically obtained from a target, combined, they provide a three-dimensional representation of the brain.

Direct Methods: EEG & MEG

It is known that active neurons generate electric

currents (action potentials propagated by axons, post-synaptic potentials that be exiters or inhibitors). The variations of the post-synaptic electric currents generate variants of magnetic field. The variation of these post-synaptic electric currents and magnetic fields are basically *direct methods of brain imaging* (electroencephalography or EEG and *magnet0-electroencephalography* or MEG). But active neuron consumes energy and oxygen. It requires a local increase in blood flow. The methods of brain imaging based on these metabolic changes constitute the second major category of methods. This is functional magnetic resonance imaging (fMRI) and positron emission tomography (PET). These are called *indirect methods* because the extent of these metabolic changes is only an indirect method of the electrical activity of neurons.

EEG & MEG

The data from EEG and MEG directly reflect the neuronal activity. It is the activity-more precisely post-synaptic potential (PSP) of neuron populations (100,000 to 1 million) active at the same time (since the PSP lasts only a few tens of milliseconds) in a space of a few cubic millimetres of the cortex.

EEG. EEG activity is recorded using signal-receiving electrodes placed on the surface of the scalp. The signal must be amplified to be detectable. At present there are helmets, provided with 32, 64, 128 electrodes which must be placed on the head of the subject. When the helmet contains more electrodes, the spatial precision of regions explored is greater.

The signal thus recorded is presented in the form of a succession of short waves, the spontaneous or "rough" EEG, which differ in sequence (in hertz) and amplitude (in microvolts) of rhythms alpha, beta, theta, etc. that can be related with levels of sleep and waking. It is important to note that the frequency around 40 Hz is significant with respect to cognitive activities.

MEG. The MEG technique records, near the scalp, the cerebral magnetic fields produced by the same synaptic current as those that are recorded by EEG. This is a much more recent technique than EEG, but require much more complicated equipment. The equipment comprises magnetic field detectors, made up of a bobbin of conducting a metal wire (magnetometers). These are in a superconductor environment, without resistance. This allows the fields generated (which are very weak) to be detected. The superconductor environment is possible only if the magnetometers are plunged in liquid helium cooled to -270°C. This is the reason the equipment includes a large tube located above the head of the subject in which the detectors are coupled with a device to ensure cooling.

The Evoked Potentials (Eps). When subjects perceive stimuli or are engaged with cognitive tasks, the perception generate potentials of very low amplitude (a few microvolts) that are not visible on the track of the rough EEG (the amplitude of which is several tens of microvolts); reproducible from one assay to another. These Eps are linked to the event (by the stimuli or by the cognitive treatments implicated in the tasks). Because of the reproducible character of these potentials (such EP occurs always in the same region and in the same range of post-stimulus latency for a single situation), it is possible to visualize them, and thus subsequently to measure them, using the techniques of averages.

The principle of averages is the following: the EEG is

continuously recorded (on the computer) while the subject is given a succession of stimuli, which could be different, calling for one or more responses. Using an adapted software program, portions of the EEG are then grouped (on a time window chosen beforehand).

Indirect Methods: PET & fMRI

The methods of PET and fMRI both founded on blood flow in the brain (thus metabolic methods), differ in their principle in the variable measured and in their application.

PET (Positron Emission Tomography)

PET is a brain-imaging technique that has been widely used in biopsychological research because it provides images of brain activity rather than brain structure. In one common version of PET, radioactive 2-deoxyglucose (2-DG) is injected into the subject's carotid artery (an artery of the neck the feeds the cerebral hemisphere). Because of its similarity to glucose, the primary metabolic fuel of the brain, 2-DG is rapidly taken up by active (energy-consuming) neurons. However, unlike glucose, 2-DG cannot be metabolized; it therefore accumulates in active neurons until it is gradually broken down. Each PET scan is the image of the levels of radioactivity (indicated by colour coding) in various parts of one horizontal level of the brain. Thus, if a PET scan is taken of a subject who engages in an activity such as reading for about 30 seconds after the 2-DG injection, the resulting scan will indicate the brain level that were most active during the 30 seconds of activity. Usually, several different levels of the brain are scanned so that the extent of brain activity can be better assessed.

PET scans are not images of the brain. Each PET scan is merely a coloured map of the amount of radioactivity in each of the tiny cubic volume that compose the scan.

Functional Magnetic Resonance (fMRI)

Functional magnetic resonance arose from anatomic magnetic resonance imaging (aMRI), conceived in 1970 to study the constituents of cerebral tissue.

Magnetic resonance is based on the magnetic properties of hemoglobin, which differ slightly according to whether this molecule is linked to oxygen or otherwise. The synaptic activity consumes oxygen, which leads to a local increase in blood flow. This is the BOLD (blood oxygen level-dependent) response. In effect, the input of oxygen necessary for the activity is possible only by means of the increase of blood circulation, which results from vasodilation of surrounding arterioles. The blood thus brought near the active synapses is charged with oxygen. In other words, it is rich in oxyhemoglobin. BOLD response is detectable only for some hundreds of milliseconds after the synaptic activity. After that, the blood which is discharged of its oxygen, increases in deoxyhemoglobin concentration before it returns to normal.

Using fMRI it is possible to visualize the contrasts between the regions in which blood flow increases, which are rich in oxyhemoglobin and the regions in which the blood flow does not vary, by means of the magnetic properties of the iron contained in the hemoglobin. In fact, the oxyhemoglobin (iron associated with oxygen) is diamagnetic. When the subject is placed in the equipment generating the magnetic field, each molecule of deoxyhemoglobin causes a local disturbance of the homogeneity of the magnetic field, which leads to dephasing of spins and reduces the MRI signal. When there is cerebral activation, these small heterogeneities of the magnetic field are reduced and the MRI signal increases. The deoxyhemoglobin is thus an endogenous magnetic tracer.

Concluding Remarks

Unlike PET, fMRI is a non-invasive method since it uses an endogenous signal. Its spatial resolution is high (of the order of millimeters for fMRI). Its temporal resolution is of the order of some hundreds of milliseconds. Obviously of much lower quality than that of PET. It is thus an excellent method for visualization of the brain in activity. However, it cannot be used to follow in detail the temporal organization of cerebral activities in association with the progression of cognitive processes.

If EEG and MEG are methods of choice for chronometry of mental operations characteristics of cognitive functions, fMRI is adequate for the location of active cerebral structures. The future lies in a combination of these two types of methods.

Chapter 4

Neuro-Anatomy

In order to understand what the brain does, it is first necessary to understand what it is – to know the names and locations of its major parts and how they are connected to one another.

General Layout of the Nervous System

Divisions of the Nervous System

The vertebrate nervous system is composed of two divisions: the central nervous system and the peripheral nervous system. Roughly speaking, the **central nervous system (CNS)** is the division of the nervous system that is located within the skull and spine; the **peripheral nervous system (PSN)** is the division that is located outside the skull and spine.

The central nervous system is composed of two divisions: the brain and the spinal cord. The *brain* is the part of the CNS that is located in the skull; the *spinal cord* is the part that is located in the spine.

The peripheral nervous system is also composed of two divisions: the somatic nervous system is also composed of two divisions: the somatic nervous system and the autonomic nervous system. The **somatic nervous system (SNS)** is the part of the PNS that interacts with the external environment. It is composed of **afferent nerves** that carry sensory signals from the skin, skeletal muscles, joints, eyes, ears, and so on, to the central nervous system, and **efferent nerves** that carry motor signals from the central nervous system to the skeletal muscles. The **autonomic nervous system (ANS)** is the part of the peripheral nervous system that regulates the body's internal environment. It is composed of afferent nerves that carry sensory signals from internal organs to the CNS and efferent nerves that carry motor signal from the CNS to internal organs.

The autonomic nervous system has two kinds of efferent nerves: sympathetic nerves and parasympathetic nerves. The **sympathetic nerves** are those autonomic motor nerves that project from the CNS in the *lumbar* (small of the back) and *thoracic* (chest area) regions of the spinal cord. The **parasympathetic nerves** are those autonomic motor nerves that project from the brain and *sacral* (lower back) region of the spinal cord.

The conventional view of the respective functions of the sympathetic and parasympathetic systems stresses three important principles: (1) that sympathetic nerves stimulate, organize, and mobilize energy resources in threatening situations, whereas parasympathetic nerves act to conserve energy; (2) that each autonomic target organ receives opposing sympathetic and parasympathetic input, and its activity is thus controlled by relative levels of sympathetic and parasympathetic activity; and (3) that sympathetic changes are indicative of psychological arousal, whereas parasympathetic changes are indicative of psychological relaxation.

Figure 1 summarizes the major divisions of the nervous system. Notice that the nervous system is a "system of twos."

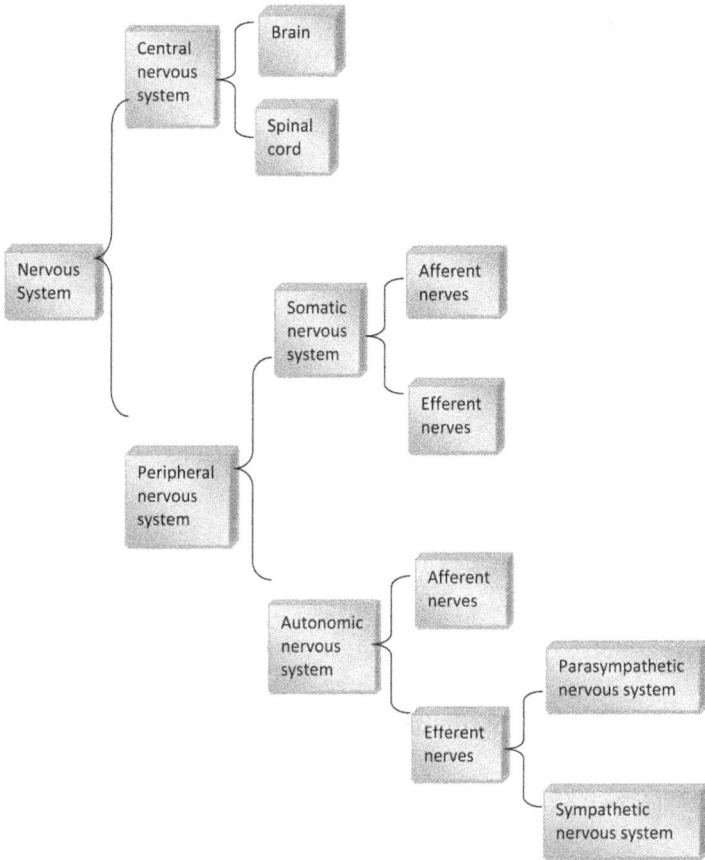

Figure 1: The major divisions of the nervous system

Cells of the Nervous System

Most of the cells of the nervous system are of two fundamentally different types: neurons and glial cells.

Anatomy of Neurons

Neurons are cells that are specialized for the reception, conduction, and transmission of electrochemical signals. They come in an incredible variety of shapes and sizes.

External Anatomy of Neurons

Figure 2 is an illustration of the major external features of one type of neuron. For your convenience, the definition of each feature is included in the illustration.

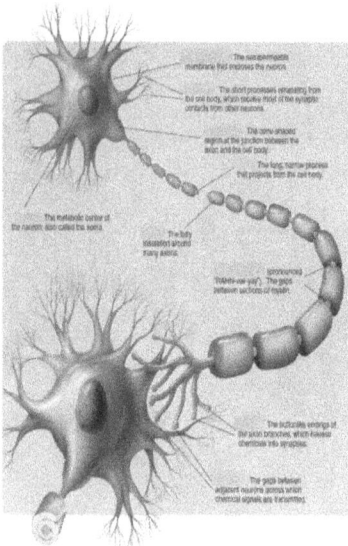

Fig: AXON (EXTERNAL)   Fig: AXON (INTERNAL)

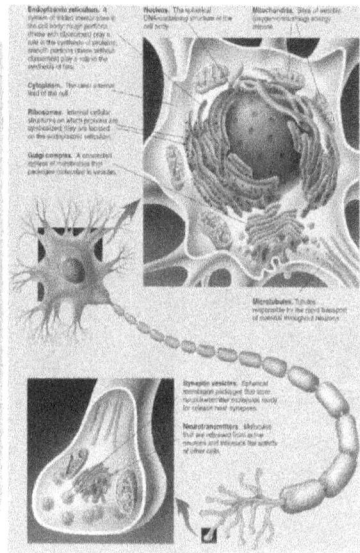

Internal Anatomy of Neurons

Figure 3 is an illustration of the major internal features of one type of neuron. Again, the definition of each feature is included in the illustration.

Neuron Cell Membrane

The neuron cell membrane is composed of a *lipid*

bilayer – two layers of fat molecules. Embedded in the lipid bilayer are numerous protein molecules that are the basis of many of the cell membrane's functional properties. Some membrane proteins are *channel proteins,* through which certain molecules can pass; others are *signal proteins,* which transfer a signal to the inside of the neuron when particular molecules bind to them on the outside of the membrane.

In general, there are two kinds of gross neural structures in the nervous system: those composed primarily of cell bodies and those composed primarily of axons. In the central nervous system, clusters of cell bodies are called **nuclei** (singular *nucleus*); in the peripheral nervous system, they are called **ganglia** (singular *ganglion*). (Note that the word *nucleus* has two different neuroanatomical meanings; it is a structure in the neuron cell body and a cluster of cell bodies in the CNS.) In the central nervous system, bundles of axons are called **tracts**; in the peripheral nervous system, they are called **nerves.**

Glial Cells

Neurons are not the only cells in the nervous system; the others are called **glial cells.** Glial cells outnumber neurons by 10 to 1.

The Spinal Cord

In cross section, it is apparent that the spinal cord comprises two different areas: an inner H-shaped core of gray matter and a surrounding area of white matter. *Gray matter* is composed largely of cell bodies and unmyelinated interneurons, whereas *white matter* is composed largely of myelinated axons. (It is the myelin that gives the white matter its glossy white sheen). The two dorsal arms of the spinal gray matter are called the **dorsal horns,** and the two ventral arms are called the **ventral horns.**

Pairs of *spinal nerves* are attached to the spinal cord-one on the left and one on the right-at 31 different levels of the spine. Each of these 62 spinal nerves divides as it nears the cord, and its axons are joined to the cord via one of two roots: the *dorsal root* or the *ventral root.*

All dorsal root axons, whether somatic or autonomic, are sensory (afferent) unipolar neurons with their cell

The Five Major Divisions of the Brain

A necessary step in learning to live in an unfamiliar city is learning the names and locations of its major neighborhoods or districts. Those who possess this information can easily communicate the general location of any destination in the city.

To understand why the brain is considered to be composed of five divisions, it is necessary to understand its early development. In the vertebrate embryo, the tissue that eventually develops into the CNS is recognizable as a fluid-filled tube (see figure 4). The first indications of the developing brain are three swellings that occur at the anterior end of this tube. These three swellings eventually develop into the adult *forebrain, midbrain, and hindbrain.*

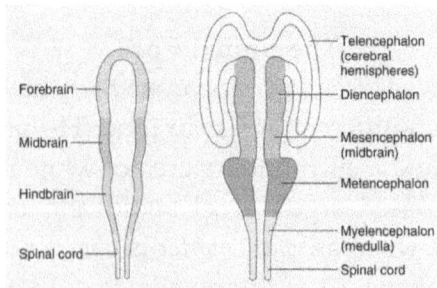

Forebrain
Midbrain
Hindbrain
Spinal cord

Telencephalon (cerebral hemispheres)
Diencephalon
Mesencephalon (midbrain)
Metencephalon
Myelencephalon (medulla)
Spinal cord

Fig: Early Mammalian Brain

Before birth, the initial three swellings in the neural tube become five (see figure 4). This occurs because the forebrain swelling grows into two different swellings, and so does the hindbrain swelling. From anterior to posterior, the five swellings that compose the developing brain at birth are the *telencephalon,* the *diencephalon,* the *mesencephalon* (or midbrain), the *metencephalon,* and the *myelencephalon* (*encephalon* means "within the head"). These swellings ultimately develop into the five divisions of the adult brain.

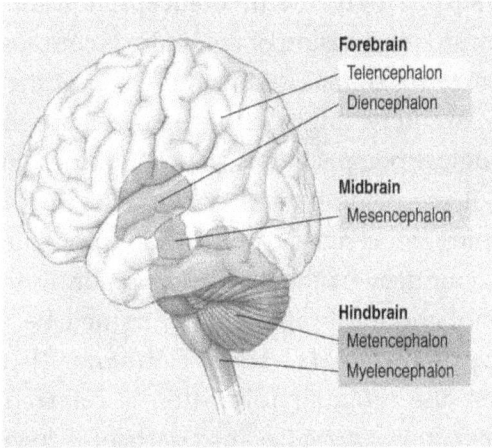

Fig: Divisions of Adult Human Brain

Figure 5 illustrates the locations of the telencephalon, diencephalon, mesencephalon, metencephalon, and myelencephalon in the adult human brain. Notice that in humans, as in other higher vertebrates, the telencephalon (the left and right *cerebral hemispheres*) undergoes the greatest growth during development. The other four divisions of the brain are often referred to collectively as the **brain stem** – the stem on which the cerebral hemispheres sit. The myelencephalon is often referred to as the *medulla.*

Major Structures of the Brain

Now that you have learned the five major divisions of the brain, it is time to introduce you to their major structures. The survey begins with brain structures in the myelencephalon, then ascends through the other divisions to the telencephalon.

Myelencephalon (Medulla)

Not surprisingly, the **myelencephalon** (or **medulla**), the most posterior division of the brain, is composed largely of tracts carrying signals between the rest of the brain and the body. An interesting part of the myelencephalon from a psychological perspective is the **reticular formation** (see Figure 6). It is a complex network of about 100 tiny nuclei that occupies the central core of the brain stem from the posterior boundary of the myelencephalon to the anterior boundary of the midbrain. It is so named because of its netlike appearance (*reticulum* means "little net"). Sometimes, the reticular formation is referred to as the *reticular activating system* because parts of it seem to play a role in arousal. However, the various nuclei of the reticular formation are involved in a variety of functions – including sleep, attention, movement, the maintenance of muscle tone, and various cardiac, circulatory, and respiratory reflexes. Accordingly, referring to this collection of nuclei as a system can be misleading.

Metencephalon

The **metencephalon**, like the myelencephalon, houses many ascending and descending tracts and part of the reticular formation. These structures create a bulge, called the **pons**, on the brain stem's ventral surface. The pons is one major division of the metencephalon; the other is the cerebellum (little brain) – see Figure 6. The **cerebellum** is the large, convoluted structure on the brain stem's dorsal surface. It is an important sensorimotor structure; cerebellar damage eliminates the ability to precisely control one's movements and to adapt them to changing conditions. However, the fact that cerebellar damage also produces a variety of cognitive deficits suggests that the functions of the cerebellum are not restricted to sensorimotor control.

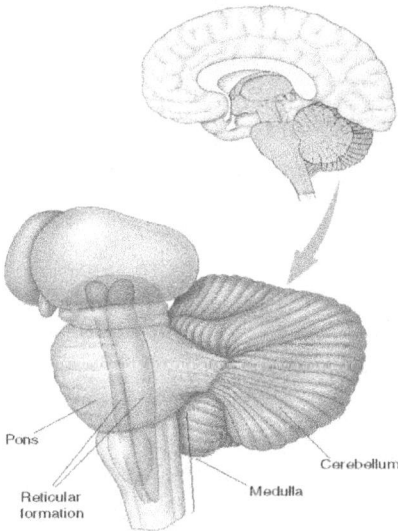

Fig: Myelencephalon (Medulla) and Metencephalon

Mesencephalon (Midbrain)

The **mesencephalon,** like the metencephalon, has two divisions. The two divisions of the mesencephalon are the tectum and the tegmentum (see Figure 7). The **tectum** (roof) is the dorsal surface of the midbrain. In mammals, the tectum is composed of two pairs of bumps, the *colliculi* (little hills). The posterior pair, called the **inferior colliculi,** have an auditory function; the anterior pair, called the **superior colliculi,** have a visual function. In lower vertebrates, the function of the tectum is entirely visual; thus, the tectum is referred to as the *optic tectum.*

The **tegmentum** is the division of the mesencephalon ventral to the tectum. In addition to the reticular formation and tracts of passage, the tegmentum contains three colorful structures that are of particular interest to biopsychologists: the periaqueductal gray, the substantia nigra, and the red nucleus (see Figure). The **periaqueductal gray** is the gray matter situated around the **cerebral aqueduct,** the duct connecting the third and fourth ventricles; it is of special interest because of its role in mediating the analgesic (pain-reducing) effects of opiate drugs. The **substantia nigra** (black substance) and the **red nucleus** are both important components of the sensorimotor system.

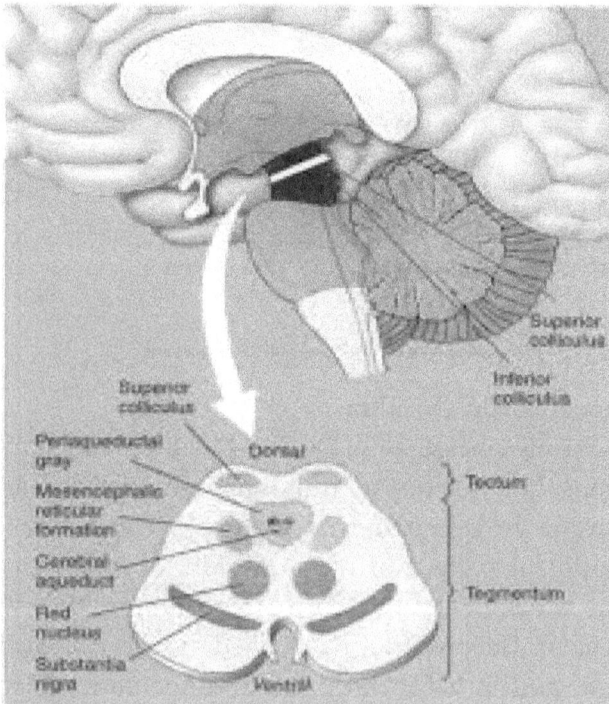

Fig: Mesencephalon (Mid Brain)

Diencephalon

The **diencephalon** is composed of two structures: the thalamus and the hypothalamus (see Figure 8). The **thalamus** is the large, two-lobed structure that constitutes the top of the brain stem. One lobe sits on each side of the third ventricle, and the two lobes are joined by the **massa intermedia**, which runs through the ventricle. Visible on the surface of the thalamus are white *lamina* (layers) that are composed of myelinated axons.

Diencephalon

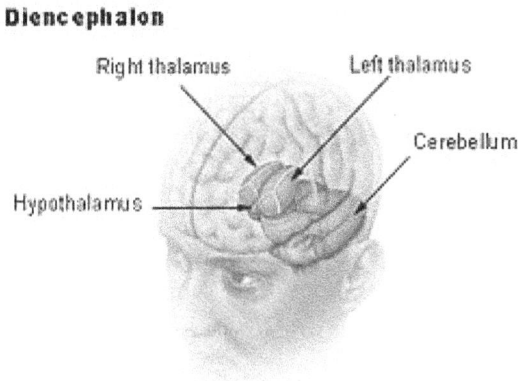

Fig: Diencephalon

The thalamus comprises many different pairs of nuclei, most of which project to the cortex. Some are *sensory relay nuclei* – nuclei that receive signals from sensory receptors, process them, and then transmit them to the appropriate areas of sensory cortex. For example, the **lateral geniculate nuclei,** the **medial geniculate nuclei,** and the **ventral posterior nuclei** are important relay stations in the visual, auditory, and somatosensory systems, respectively.

The **hypothalamus** is located just below the anterior

thalamus (*hypo* means "below") – see Figure 8. It plays an important role in the regulation of several motivated behaviors. It exerts its effects in part by regulating the release of hormones from the **pituitary gland,** which dangles from it on the ventral surface of the brain. The literal meaning of *pituitary gland* is "snot gland"; it was discovered in a gelatinous state behind the nose of an unembalmed cadaver and was incorrectly assumed to be the main source of nasal mucus.

In addition to the pituitary gland, two other structures appear on the inferior surface of the hypothalamus: the optic chiasm and the mammillary bodies (see Figure). The **optic chiasm** is the point at which the *optic nerves* from each eye come together. The X shape is created because some of the axons of the optic nerve **decussate** (cross over to the other side of the brain) via the optic chiasm. The decussating fibers are said to be **contralateral** (projecting from one side of the body to the other), and the non-decussating fibers are said to be **ipsilateral** (staying on the same side of the body). The **mammillary bodies,** which are often considered to be part of the hypothalamus, are a pair of spherical nuclei located on the inferior surface of the hypothalamus, just behind the pituitary.

Telencephalon

The **telencephalon,** the largest division of the human brain, mediates the brain's most complex functions. It initiates voluntary movement, interprets sensory input, and mediates complex cognitive processes such as learning, speaking, and problem solving.

Cerebral Cortex. The cerebral hemispheres are covered by a layer of tissue called the **cerebral cortex** (cerebral bark).

In humans, the cerebral cortex is deeply convoluted (furrowed) – see Figure 9 & 10. The *convolutions* have the effect of increasing the amount of cerebral cortex without increasing the over-all volume of the brain. Not all mammals have convoluted cortexes; most mammals are *lissencephalic* (smooth-brained). It was once believed that the number and size of cortical convolutions determined a species' intellectual capacities; however, the number and size of cortical convolutions appear to be related more to body size. Every large mammal has an extremely convoluted cortex.

The large furrows in a convoluted cortex are called **fissures,** and the small ones are called *sulci* (singular *sulcus*). The ridges between fissures and sulci are called **gyri** (singular *gyrus*). It is apparent in Figure that the cerebral hemispheres are almost completely separated by the largest of the fissures: the **longitudinal fissure.** The cerebral hemispheres are directly connected by only a few tracts spanning the longitudinal fissure; these hemisphere-connecting tracts are called **cerebral commissures.** The largest cerebral commissure, the **corpus callosum,** is clearly visible in Figure.

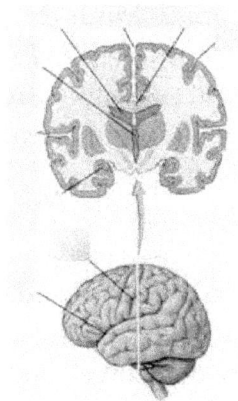

The two major landmarks on the lateral surface of each hemisphere are the **central fissure** and the **lateral fissure.** These fissures partially divide each hemisphere into four lobes: the **frontal lobe,** the **parietal lobe** (pronounced "pa-RYE-e-tal"), the **temporal lobe,** and the **occipital lobe** (pronounced "ok-SIP-i-tal"). Among the largest gyri are the **precentral gyri,** which contain motor cortex; the **postcentral gyri,** which contain somatosensory (body-sensation) cortex; and the **superior temporal gyri,** which contain auditory cortex. The function of occipital cortex is entirely visual.

About 90% of human cerebral cortex is **neocortex** (new cortex); that is, it is six-layered cortex of relatively recent evolution. By convention, the layers of neocortex are numbered I through VI, starting at the surface. Figure illustrates two adjacent sections of neocortex. One has been stained with a Nissl stain to reveal the number and shape of its cell bodies; the other has been stained with a Golgi stain to reveal the silhouettes of a small proportion of its neurons.

Three important characteristics of neocortical anatomy are apparent. First, it is apparent that there are two fundamentally different kinds of cortical neurons: pyramidal (pyramid-shaped) cells and stellate (star-shaped) cells. **Pyramidal cells** are large multipolar neurons with pyramid-shaped cell bodies, a large dendrite called an *apical dendrite* that extends from the apex of the pyramid straight toward the cortex surface, and a very long axon. In contrast, **stellate cells** are small star-shaped interneurons (neurons with short axons or no axon). Second, it is apparent that the six layers of neocortex differ from one another in terms of the size and density of their cell bodies and the relative proportion of pyramidal and stellate cell bodies that they contain. Third, it is apparent that many long axons and dendrites course vertically (i.e., at right angles to the cortical layers) through the neocortex. This vertical flow of information is the basis of the neocortex's **columnar organization;** neurons in a given vertical column of neocortex often form a mini-circuit that performs a single function. Fourth, although all neocortex is six-layered, there are variations in the layers from area to area (Figure 11). For example, because the stellate cells of layer IV are specialized for receiving sensory signals from the thalamus, layer IV is extremely thick in areas of sensory cortex. Conversely, because the pyramidal cells of layer V conduct signals from the neocortex to the brain stem and spinal cord, layer V is extremely thick in areas of motor cortex.

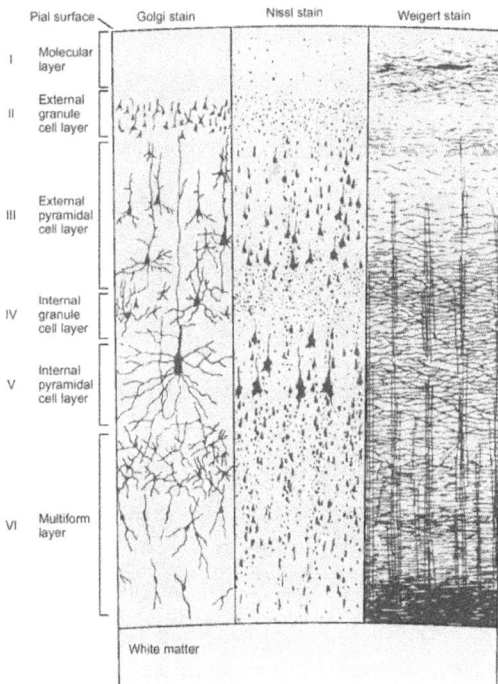

Fig: Six Layers of Neocortex

The **hippocampus** is one important area of cortex that is not neocortex – it has only three layers. The hippocampus is located at the medial edge of the cerebral cortex as it folds back on itself in the medial temporal lobe (see Figure 12). This folding produces a shape that is, in cross section, somewhat reminiscent of a sea horse (*hippocampus* means "sea horse").

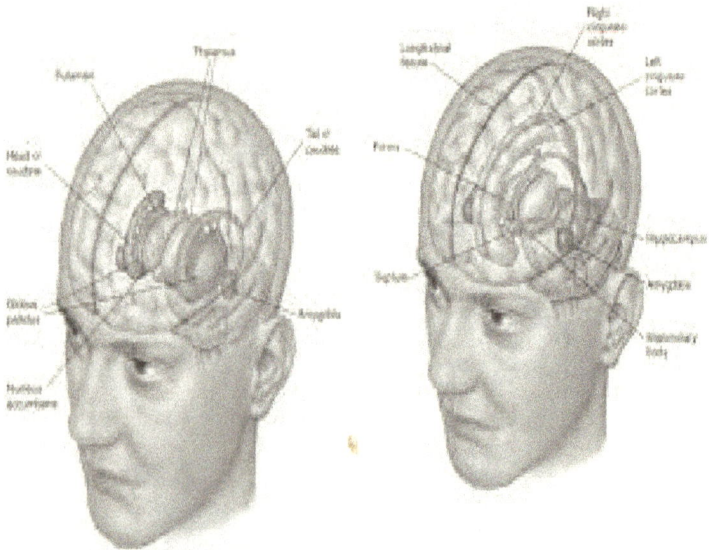

Fig: Major Structures

The Limbic System and the Basal Ganglia. Although much of the subcortical portion of the telencephalon is taken up by axons projecting to and from the neocortex, there are several large subcortical nuclear groups. Some of them are considered to be part of either the *limbic system* or the *basal ganglia motor system*. Don't be misled by the word *system* in these contexts; it implies a level of certainty that is unwarranted. It is not entirely clear exactly what these hypothetical systems do, exactly which structures should be included in them, or even whether it is appropriate to view them as unitary systems. Nevertheless, if not taken too literally, the concepts of *limbic system* and *basal ganglia motor system* provides a useful means of conceptualizing the organization of the subcortex.

The **limbic system** is a circuit of midline structures that circle the thalamus (*limbic* means "ring"). The limbic system is involved in the regulation of motivated behaviors – including the four Fs of motivation: fleeing, feeding, fighting, and sexual behavior. (This joke is as old as biopsychology itself, but it is a good one). In addition to several structures about which you have already read (e.g., the mammillary bodies and the hippocampus), major structures of the limbic system include the amygdala, the fornix, the cingulate cortex, and the septum.

Let's begin tracing the limbic circuit (see Figure) at the **amygdala** – the almond-shaped nucleus in the anterior temporal lobe (*amygdala* means "almond" and is pronounced "a-MIG-dah-lah"). Posterior to the amygdala is the hippocampus, which runs beneath the thalamus in the medial temporal lobe. Next in the ring are the cingulate cortex and the fornix. The **cingulate cortex** is the large area of neocortex in the **cingulate gyrus** on the medial surface of the cerebral hemispheres, just superior to the corpus callosum; it encircles the dorsal thalamus (*cingulate* means "encircling"). The **fornix,** the major tract of the limbic system, also encircles the dorsal thalamus; it leaves the dorsal end of the hippocampus and sweeps forward in an arc coursing along the superior surface of the third ventricle and terminating in the septum and mammillary bodies (*fornix* means "arc"). The **septum** is a midline nucleus that is located at the anterior tip of the cingulate cortex. Several tracts connect the septum and mammillary bodies with the amygdala and hippocampus. Thereby completing the limbic ring.

The **basal ganglia** are illustrated in Figure. As we did with the limbic system, let's begin our examination of the basal ganglia with the amygdala, which is considered to be part of both systems. Sweeping out of each amygdala, first in a posterior direction and then in an anterior direction, is the long tail-like **caudate** (*caudate* means "tail-like"). Each caudate forms an almost complete circle; in its center, connected to it by a series of fiber bridges, is the **putamen** (pronounced "pew-TAY-men"). Together, the caudate and the putamen, which both have a striped appearance, are known as the **striatum** (striped structure). The remaining structure of the basal ganglia is the pale circular structure known as the **globus pallidus** (pale globe). The globus pallidus is located medial to the putamen, between the putamen and the thalamus.

The basal ganglia play a major role in the performance of voluntary motor responses. Of particular interest is a pathway that projects to the striatum from the substantia nigra of the midbrain. *Parkinson's disease*, a disorder that is characterized by rigidity, tremors, and poverty of voluntary movement, is associated with the deterioration of this pathway.

Table summarizes the major brain divisions and structures.

	Cerebral cortex	Neocortex
		Hippocampus
	Major fissures	Central fissure
		Lateral fissure
		Longitudinal fissure

		Precentral gyrus
	Major gyri	Postcentral gyrus
		Superior temporal gyrus
		Cingulate gyrus
Telencephalon	Four lobes	Frontal lobe
		Temporal lobe
		Parietal lobe
		Occipital lobe
	Limbic system	Amygdala
		Hippocampus
		Fornix
		Cingulate cortex
		Septum
		Mammillary bodies
	Basal ganglia	Amygdala
		Caudate ⎤ Striatum
		Putamen ⎦
		Globus pallidus
	Cerebral commissures	Corpus callosum
	Thalamus	Massa intermedia
		Lateral geniculate nuclei
		Medial geniculate nuclei
Diencephalon		Ventral posterior nuclei
	Hypothalamus	Mammillary bodies
	Optic chiasm	
	Pituitary gland	
	Tectum	Superior colliculi
		Interior colliculi
		Reticular formation
Mesencephalon		Cerebral aqueduct
	Tegmentum	Periaqueductal gray
		Substantia nigra
		Red nucleus
	Reticular formation	
Metencephalon	Pons	
	Cerebellum	
Myelencephalon or Medulla	Reticular formation	

Chapter 5

Neurochemistry

Despite the extraordinary sophistication of modern cars, there are two vital fluids that must be in there for the car to run at all. One is some refined volatile substance – petrol or diesel. The other is oil. The volatile substance needs a spark to create the explosion that releases energy to drive a piston or spin the jet blades. Oil doesn't need a spark, but its capacity to lubricate is vital in making the systems work well.

Then there are some more fluids that make the car function well – coolant, hydraulic fluids for brakes and steering, screen-wash water, and so on – a surprising number that most days we take for granted.

So it is with the brain and body. There are two major chemical systems that control our behavior and wellbeing. One predominates in the brain and, just like petrol in an engine, requires electricity to make it work. It is the neurochemistry of the brain. The other, more like oil, predominates in the rest of the body, circulates in the blood, is managed by the endocrine glands and is called the endocrine system. Adrenalin is one endocrine chemical or, because it affects the brain, is also referred to as a neuroendocrine (nerves and hormones) chemical. In all kinds of ways endocrines oil the works and make the body efficient for whatever the task is that is in hand. They are vital to making the system work. They send messages around the body, telling it what to do.

The two systems interact in humans in ways which are so complex and multi-layered that we are not even close to fully understanding them. Although our basic system of electrical signaling might be recognizably akin to that of a simple animal like the squid, the evolutionary demands that led to the growth in number of neurons and connections and dense folding of the mammalian, then human, brain also led to more signaling mechanisms and much more nuanced relationships between them.

The two systems interact together, of course, not only in times of ordinary demand but also when unusual stress, load or demand is placed upon the system – just as in a car going continuously uphill in excessively hot and dusty conditions. If the systems have been geared to withstand extreme stress then, well prepared, they will. But if the demands are too great, some part of the system will break down.

Neurochemistry – the specialism in science that is concerned with the chemistry of the nervous system – knows that there are over 100 different chemicals at work in the brain. For our purposes, though, it is useful to know that the main chemicals that control behavior are either neurotransmitters or hormones.

Neurotransmitters are of two kinds. They stimulate or they calm. They relay signals between nerve cells (neurons). The brain uses neurotransmitters to trigger hormones to tell your heart to beat, your lungs to breathe, and your stomach to digest. They can also affect mood, sleep, concentration, weight, and can cause adverse symptoms when they are out of balance. Neurotransmitter levels can be depleted in many ways. Stress, poor diet, neurotoxins, genetic predisposition, drugs (prescription and recreational), including alcohol, nicotine and caffeine usage can cause these levels to be out of optimal range.

NEUROTRANSMITTERS AND HORMONES

The main neurotransmitters are:

Dopamine	*Serotonin*
Oxytocin	*Noradrenalin*

The main hormones are:

Cortisol	*Adrenalin*
Testosterone	*Estrogen/progesterone*

They work together. Earlier we likened neurotransmitters to petrol in an engine and hormones to oil and the other crucial fluids that make brakes work or power-assist the moving parts. Neurotransmitters need a spark – an electrical current generated in a nerve cell – to make them effective. Hormones are released by the demands of neurochemicals signals directly into the bloodstream from ductless glands around the body and, like all the fluids in a car, are necessary in the right quantities and in the right places to make things work effectively.

One way of thinking about the neurotransmitters is that they act directly on the emotions and trigger the hormones: whilst the hormones act directly on the body. Of course in practice both are integrated. That might be a bit simplistic, but it is not a bad staring point.

HORMONES

Hormones are chemicals that carry messages from glands to cells within tissues or organs in the body. They also maintain chemical levels in the bloodstream to help achieve *homeostasis*, which is a state of stability or balance within the body. They are part of the endocrine ("within the secreting") system. Glands manufacture hormones.

These chemicals circulate freely in the bloodstream, waiting to be recognized by a target cell responding to an instruction from a neurotransmitter signal. The target cell has a receptor that can be activated only by a specific type of hormone, after which the cell knows to start a certain function within its walls. *Genes* might get activated, for example, or energy production resumed.

Emotions

Emotions are the irreducible basics of making sense of anything. Combined together, they create feelings. Although there is a good deal of debate as to how many emotions there actually are, the accumulated evidence (based on Goleman's *Emotional Intelligence*) favors eight. Think of them like primary colors. Three primary colors make the whole of the color spectrum. Eight primary emotions make the whole emotional spectrum of the feeling system.

Of the eight primary emotions, the five survival emotions (fear, anger, disgust, shame and sadness) involve the release of cortisol. They are likely to be represented in the autonomic nervous system (ANS) that is functioning largely below the conscious level, and are all escape/avoidance/survival emotions, generating complex behaviors.

The two attachment emotion spectrums (love/trust and joy/excitement) are mediated by the effects of oxytocin, dopamine and noradrenalin on brain receptors.

One emotion, surprise, is a "potentiator" that can flip response states from attachment to survival or survival to attachment. Noradrenalin intensifies the effects of many other neurochemicals and probably underlies surprise.

Sometimes, of course, all eight emotions can be firing simultaneously. In intense jealousy, for example, love and anger can be equally strong. When firing in competition with each other the distress can often only be relieved by violent action. It changes the emotional context, sometimes catastrophically, when the emotions themselves are in such intense opposition as they are when jealousy is raging.

It is becoming more and more widely accepted that an emotionally intelligent leader's ability to build and sustain trust leads to a business's long-term survival and success. Much as the attachment emotions build the neural architecture of our children, inspiring trust in the workplace encourages team bonding, learning and innovation. These are higher functions in the brain that demand a large proportion of its precious resources, and these resources get used up in self-preservation where the brain perceives any potential threat.

Trust

Although humans are capable of transmitting ideas and adopting innovations faster than any other species, the human brain is still shaped by evolutionary development that adapts structures rather than destroying them to build new ones. Tomorrow looks uncertain and risky and hence the brain reacts as if the future can lead to "safe" decisions, or, more worryingly, delay them. Creativity is constrained by fear of uncertainty.

In modern organizations, where it is primarily the quality of thinking and innovation that matter and where relationships with customers, suppliers and partners are key success factors, just giving orders cannot deliver the kind of performance needed. Leaders can no longer rely on hierarchical position for their power. More than ever, they need to persuade, inspire and motivate. In any case, leadership is required at all levels in an organization, not just top-down. Intelligent, highly educated, intrinsically motivated people require goals they can believe in and subscribe to. The leader nevertheless sets the cultural DNA of the organization. It's there where essential trust has to reside.

So in order for a leader to inspire and motivate, he or she has to be trusted. Trust creates an environment in which threats are reduced, and thinking and creativity are liberated. A trusted leader will be believed when they tell stories about what the future will be like, thus reducing fear and anxiety. A trusted leader with a strong emotional commitment to a cause or goal will be able to engender commitment in others. A trusted leader who takes risks and persists through difficulties will continue to be followed even when the journey seems dangerous.

Why does trust work?

Trust is a keystone of human society. It is the basis of our concept of money, our institutions of government, law and of the professions. It is trust in our social environment and institutions that permits us to expect to be fairly rewarded for our ideas and labor, to engage in commerce, to leave money in a will. Without trust, there is fear. Without trust, our basic human rights and responsibilities cannot be robust.

The reasons for the importance of trust to human societies are likely to be rooted in our need of others in order to survive. Trust is a multilayered and multidimensional concept. What most scholars seem to agree on however is that is it a mental action or state. We would further suggest that trust if the mental state of expecting fairness from the trusted.

Fairness seems to be almost instinctively available to humans as a working concept – evidenced from arguments with three-year-olds. It seems that fairness, like affiliation (social contact), is a primary need for humans. The brain responds strongly both to perceived fair and unfair actions and situations. In the first case positively, with the reward centers firing; in the latter case aversively, with those parts of the brain that respond to threats. We humans have such strong aversion to unfair behavior towards us that it overwhelms more rational assessments of the balance between gain and loss.

Trust and attachment

One chemical underlying trust is the neuropeptide oxytocin. Oxytocin levels rise significantly during childbirth and breast feeding. It is implicated in bonding between mothers and infants in mammals. It has recently been shown to be more prevalent also in new fathers, thus presumably encouraging them to develop a relationship with their baby. It underlies a wide range of human social affiliations and is popularly known as the love hormone, as it floods the brain when people fall in love and when they behave lovingly towards each other.

It has been shown experimentally that oxytocin might also increase the level of trust in the truster. Administered via a nasal spray, it caused a significant change in behavior during a game played with real money, (apparently not linked to lowering risk aversion). Trust, social affiliation and love are not the same, but an increase in oxytocin levels is implicated in all three. It is possible therefore that an increase in oxytocin is a relationship where trust was developed, would also increase affiliation.

OXYTOCIN

Produced by the hypothalamus and stored and secreted by the posterior pituitary gland, oxytocin acts primarily as a neuromodulator in the brain and is known as the bonding hormone. In an experiment where men were asked to rate pictures of 100 women on attractiveness, they rated them as more attractive after one nasal spray of oxytocin with the pictures being presented for a second time in a different order to the first time. So oxytocin underpins trust and "bonding" behavior in real life and in simulated tasks by inducing a calm, warm mood that increases tender feelings and attachment and may lead us to lower our guard.

Trust is not only restricted to relationships between people, or between people and animals. It can arise with objects such as clocks or tools, or organizations and their brands – I trust Amazon to deliver my goods, I trust Audi to have a car which keeps my family safe. It can be broken, but, with good management, it can overcome mistakes and even crises. Trust then becomes the basis of a strong emotional relationship, between people, things and concepts, in which there is a sense of safety and a reduction of fear and risk and perhaps even an increase in liking. This facilitates influence and enables creativity and innovation. Trust develops over time and is not absolute, but needs continuous care and maintenance.

Summary

Brain chemicals, and other inputs such as chemical and electrical impulses generated in the heart and the gut, underlie every single action of everyday life. All thoughts, feelings and moods are emergent. In the way that experience shapes the growing brain, so experience also makes chemical patterns and in turn the chemical patterns define our behavior and expectations. As humans we have our own unique chemical patterning in just the same way that we have our own individual way of walking, speaking, laughing and everything else that makes us the individual that we are. Knowing the effect of the neurochemicals on behavior and what impact it is having on others: and consider what chemistry he or she wishes to trigger in reports. The neurochemistry of others' brains is being triggered in any event by what a leader does and doesn't do. Knowledge might make that a more efficient and deliberate process. Recognizing the physiology, managing it and creating the conditions for success in the environment we operate and interact in are important tips.

Actions and reflections

- What did people do before we could speak? Ask for feedback on the gestures, mannerisms and noises you may make without even realizing it. You can do this with an executive coach or someone else that you trust. Things as subtle as throat-clearing, an overly firm handshake or shrugging could be perceived negatively by others. Knowing how others perceive you will give you some material for evolving your emotional intelligence and physicality positively.

- Work on empathy by imagining – mentally and physically – how it would feel to be another person's shoes. We respond to micro-muscular changes in other people's faces and simulating these ourselves can help us to imagine how they may be feeling. Pay closer attention to people's eyes narrowing, jaw clenching or flinching.

- Whilst looking in the mirror each morning, pause and consider the face looking back at you. Pause, and ask:
  - Are these the facial expressions I want to represent me today?
  - What emotions or states is your face conveying: confidence, fear, interest, indifference?
  - People will pick up on micro-muscular changes in your face. What impact will it have upon them?

Chapter 6

Planning

E xecuting a plan and regulating a response thus executed is closer to the general function of an executive. Planning or problem solving (used interchangeably) involves at least four distinct activities:

- Finding a problem
- Generating strategies for its solution
- Selecting an appropriate strategy
- Executing a planned action

During the execution of a planned action, *interferences* that distract the execution have to be resisted, and the execution of the plan has to be monitored, responding to feedbacks that necessitate *shifting* strategies. It is not imperative that plans have to be carried out. We are familiar with many such plans such as New Year resolutions that are seldom executed.

According to Luria (1980) the third functional unit of the brain, located in the prefrontal area of frontal lobe of the brain, synthesizes information about the outside world and is the means whereby the behaviour of the organism is regulated in conformity with the effects produced by its action. Although much advance has been made since Luria's observation, the main proposition is that the *prefrontal area is responsible to a large extent for planning and decision making.*

Executive Functions (EF) is an umbrella term for

functions including initiating, sustaining, shifting and inhibition/stopping. EF corresponds to planning, decision making, judgment, and self-perception.

Precursors

In the heyday of behaviorism, **cognitive psychology** was kept alive by a small group of psychologists studying attention and memory. The discipline has since matured and blossomed. One of the current and central concerns of cognitive science is what is called '**planning**', the psychological basis of intelligent goal-oriented behavior.

The arrival of **information theory** (Broadbent, 1958) and its use of terms like the internal characteristics of communication system opened the way for treating cognition as a subject matter for scientific study. But information theory was limited because it could not explain adequately the complex, versatile and active information processing. Humans can increase their information processing capacity (for example, by chunking), alter input, store it, recognize it, retrieve new materials beyond the information given, make decisions and translate these decisions into actions. It was necessary therefore to specify the *mediating mechanism* in order to explain how well these activities occur.

At approximately the same time, exciting developments occurred in the area of complex science. Mathematicians and computer engineers made powerful computers and created programmes that could play chess, prove theorems in logic and solve calculus problems. These solutions stimulated **artificial intelligence research**.

Newell, Shaw and Simon took the next important step forward for developing programmes that attempted to simulate human problem-solving processes in logic, trigonometry, and chess. Human being were viewed as symbol-manipulating information-processing systems that take in symbolic input and then process it further. Miller, Galanter and Pribram (1960), who are still perhaps the most influential theorists in the area of planning, argued in their seminal book '**Plans and the Structure of Behavior**' that these new ideas were compatible with psychological principle. For them, a plan is the connecting link between human processing and computer programme, as well as the missing connection between knowledge and action.

Miller et al (1960) proposed the concept of "plan" which is analogous to the program for a computer, to fill the theoretical vacuum between cognition and action. However, they opined that the reduction of Plans to computer programmes is still a hypothesis and requires further validation. The brain-computer analogy has since been one of the central problem in artificial intelligence. Miller et al emphasized the description of the structural features of behaviour as exemplified by ethologist (Tinbergen) and linguists (Chomsky). They asserted that behavior is organized simultaneously at several levels of complexity. With the hierarchical nature of behaviour as axiomatic, they defined *a plan as any hierarchical process that can control the order in which a sequence of operations is to be performed.* A plan could involve anything from a rough sketch of a course of action to a detailed specification of each operation. **It is the plan that controls human information processing and supplies pattern for essential connections between knowledge, evaluation, and action.**

How do we construct new plans? According to Miller, most plans are learned, either through imitations or through verbal instructions from others. A plan can be learned and stored as an **image** or as a part of it. The accumulated knowledge stored in images is incorporated into plans to provide a basis for guiding behaviour; images can therefore form a part of a plan. Miller also suggested that *search* is an adequate representation of most of the information processing that takes place during thinking and problem solving. The search is naturally planful. It seems that search and planning are interrelated, although distinct concepts. The use of plans and strategies is often a prerequisite for effective search in many situations.

Hayes-Roth and Hays-Roth (1979) proposed an **"Opportunistic model of planning"**. They defined planning as the predetermination of a course of action aimed at achieving some goal. According to them, planning represents the first stage of a two-stage problem-solving process. **Control**, the second step, consists of monitoring and guiding the execution of the plan to a successful conclusion.

As indicated earlier, several authors considered planning to be a part of the problem-solving process. However, recent ideas on planning suggest planning is a more pervasive, general regulating process than problem solving, with problem solving being a part of a planning process. Moreover, planning includes components that are not necessarily present in problem solving. One of these components is **anticipation**. According to Greeno, Riley and Gilman (1984), planning entails the procedure that recognize goals of different types during planning that search for action schemata with consequences that match goals that have been recognized, and that determine when planning is successfully completed. Thus planning involves the generation of anticipatory strategies.

The concept of plan and **strategy** are often used

interchangeably. Miller et al. considered strategies to be molar units of behaviour and viewed tactic as molecular units. Miller argued that plans are hierarchical in that one plan may call for the execution of a subplan which can, in turn, be part of another plan. According to this view, strategies are equivalent to subplan. But because of the hierarchical nature of the entire process, they can also be viewed as plans at some level of analysis. In sum, we could say that plans are higher units of analysis than strategies. But strategies can also be conceptualized as plans.

The PASS Theory

Based on A.R. Luria's (1980) analysis of brain structure and functioning, the Planning, Attention-Arousal, Simultaneous and Successive (PASS) model has been developed to explain the planning process (Das, 1996).

Luria (1980), the noted Russian physiologist, describes the planning process within the framework of three functional units. The function of the first unit is the regulation of cortical arousal and attention. The second unit codes information using simultaneous and successive processing. The third unit provides for planning, self-monitoring and structuring of cognitive activities.

Figure 1   **The PASS Model of Cognitive Processes**

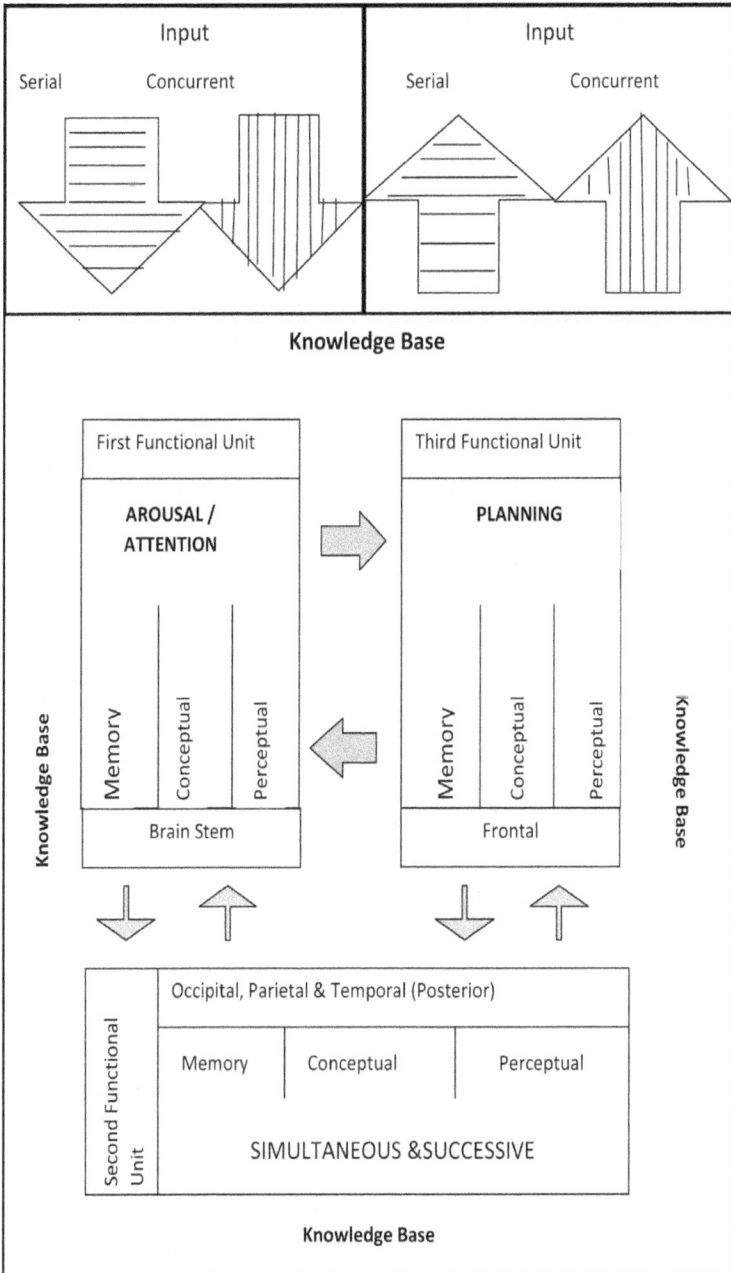

A Passage to Neuroscience of Leadership |**65**

The first functional unit of the brain, the attention-arousal system, is based mainly in the brain stem. This unit provides the brain with the appropriate level of arousal and "directive and selective attention". When multidimensional stimulus is presented, an individual is required to pay attention to only one dimension and inhibit other dimensions. The selection and allocation of attention to the relevant dimension depends on the resources of the first functional unit.

The first functional unit is not an autonomous unit, but works in cooperation with, and is regulated by cerebral cortex. This is possible through the ascending and descending systems of the reticular formation, which transmits impulses from lower parts of the brain to the cortex and vice versa (Luria). For the PASS theory, attentional-arousal function and planning are necessarily correlated since the former is under the conscious control of Planning. In other words, our plan of behavior dictates the allocation of attentional resources.

Luria's description of the second functional unit of the brain suggests that this unit is responsible for the reception, coding and storage of information arriving from the external (and partly from the internal) environment through sensory receptors. It is located in the lateral regions of the neocortex, on the convex surface of the hemispheres. This unit includes visual (occipital), auditory (temporal) and general sensory (parietal) regions. Luria described "two basic forms of integrative activity of the cerebral cortex" that take place in this unit: **simultaneous** and **successive** processing. **Simultaneous processing** is associated with the occipital-parietal areas of the brain and its essential feature is surveyability (each element is related to every other element at a given time). For example, in order to produce a diagram correctly when given the instruction, "draw a triangle above a square that is to the left a circle under a cross", the relationship among the different shapes must be correctly comprehended. **Successive processing** is associated with the fronto-temporal areas of the brain and involves the integration of stimuli into a specific serial order. For example, successive processes are involved in the decoding and production of language and speech.

The third functional unit of the brain is located in the prefrontal areas of the frontal lobes. The frontal lobes synthesize the information about the outside world. Planning processes that take place in this unit provide for the programming, regulation, and verification of behaviour and are responsible for behaviours such as asking questions, solving problems, and self-monitoring. Other responsibilities of the third functional unit include the regulation of voluntary activity, conscious impulse control, and various linguistic skills such as spontaneous conversation. The third functional unit provides for the most complex aspects of human behaviour. As Luria observes : The frontal lobes of the brain are the last acquisition of the evolutionary process and occupy nearly one-third of the brain hemisphere... They are intimately related to the reticular formation of the brain stem, being densely supplied with ascending and descending fibers... They have intimate connection with the motor cortex.... Their structures become mature only during the fourth to fifth year of life, and their development makes a rapid leap during the period which is of decisive significance for the first forms of conscious control behaviour.

Thus the PASS theory has led to the operational definition of the planning construct; it has also provided an understanding of the of the structural architecture of the planning process.

The Neuroscience of Planning

Planning is clearly associated with the frontal lobes, especially the prefrontal cortex. Neuroanatomically, this is a significant finding. The prefrontal area has the largest number of connections with other parts of the brain, including the parietal-temporal and occipital lobes, which are responsible for information coding (simultaneous and successive processing), and subcortical areas, which are responsible for the maintenance of arousal.

The three functional units of the brain work in concert to produce mental activity. The cooperation at the cognitive level is depicted by two-way arrows in Figure 1. It is stressed that although planning is a frontal lobe function, frontal lobe is not capable of independently supporting such complex activity.

Based on his extensive research on clinical symptoms resulting from brain damage, Luria identified three functional units, as indicated earlier. Luria further postulated *three basic laws* governing functional units.

The **first law** involves the hierarchical structure of the second and third functional units. The structures of second unit are subdivided into (a) the primary (projection) areas, which receive information and analyze it into its elementary components, (b) secondary (projection-association) areas, which code and convert, and (c) tertiary areas, which are responsible for symbolic schemes. The organization of third functional unit is also hierarchical. The **second law** concerns the diminishing modality character of information processing in the three zones. The primary zone retains modality characteristics (information in this zone is tagged as visual, auditory, etc). The modality information diminishes in the secondary zone, which retains some modality characteristics. The **third law** involves the progressive lateralization of functions within the brain. At the level of primary zone, there is essentially no difference in functioning of the left and right hemispheres. At the level of tertiary zone, many functions are lateralized. Speech, for example, is associated with the left hemisphere in the majority of people.

Figure 2   Frontal and Posterior / Basal Functional Systems

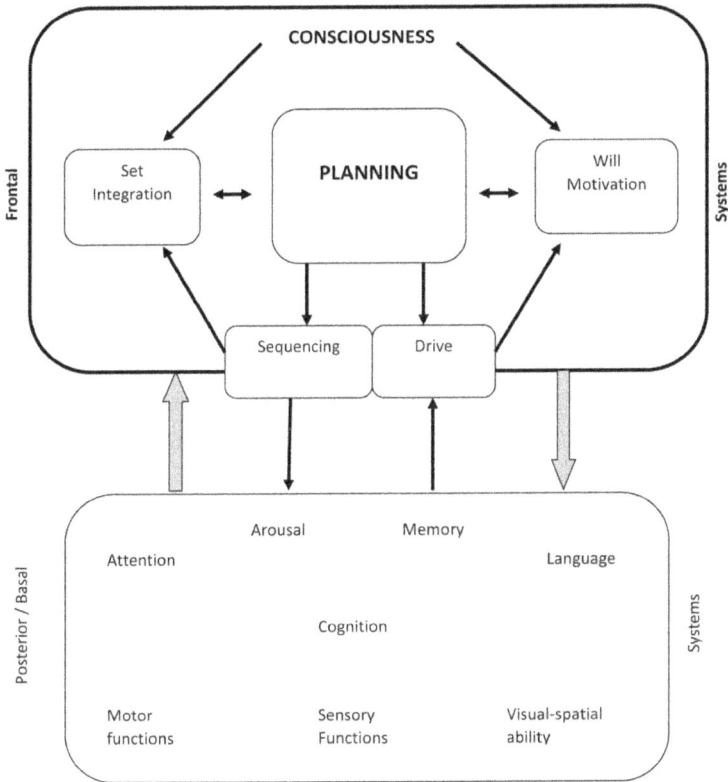

More recently Stauss and Benson combine Luria's two units and call these systems "posterior/basal functional systems". According to Stauss and Benson, these systems include a number of neural activities (see Figure 2). Each posterior/basal functional system is reciprocally connected

with the frontal area (Luria), which plays a supervisory, controlling role in their functioning. In sum, posterior/basal functional systems work under the controlling supervision of the frontal lobes whenever a task requires novel or integrated responses. They work independently of the influence of the frontal lobes whenever the response is well learned and routine.

The second block in Figure 2 consists of the frontal systems. Strauss and Benson suggested three separate "divisions" of the frontal system that are conceptually hierarchical and progressively more abstract.

The first division refers to drive and sequencing. *Sequencing* refers to organize separate bits of information into meaningful sequences. *Drive*, in turn, refers to the energizing force or need that initiates human motor and mental activity. Decrease in activity or apathy, as well as excessive activity or lack of inhibition, have been linked with frontal dysfunction. **Formation of set and integration** are closely connected to sequencing. **Will and motivation** are connected to drive.

The second division denotes planning. This division of the frontal system is formed by executive functions in general and control in particular.

The third division is termed consciousness (self-consciousness, self-awareness, self-reflectiveness), which is necessary for planning (for the regulation and control of activity in accordance with one's goals). The frontal lobes, particularly the prefrontal cortex, are essential for functions that the term consciousness refers to and which are considered the "highest" and most "human" of all mental abilities.

At an empirical level, Figure 3 identifies five components of planning: goals and objectives, anticipation, representation, execution, and regulation. All planning is guided by a goal or a purpose. Anticipation includes the ability to predict the consequences of a plan or a behaviour, the selection and shaping of environments in order to reach favorable consequences, and the selection of subgoals. Representation involves several activities: making plans, conditions for their application and setting up subgoals. Execution can consist of planning-in-action or carrying out an advance plan of action. Finally, regulation refers to the monitoring and controlling of behaviour according to the plan and revising the plan when necessary.

Empirical studies have shown that disorders of initiating, controlling, monitoring, and regulating behavior appear to be frequent after frontal lobe damage. This suggests that the frontal lobe is the center for planning behavior.

Figure 3   Planning as a Frontal System

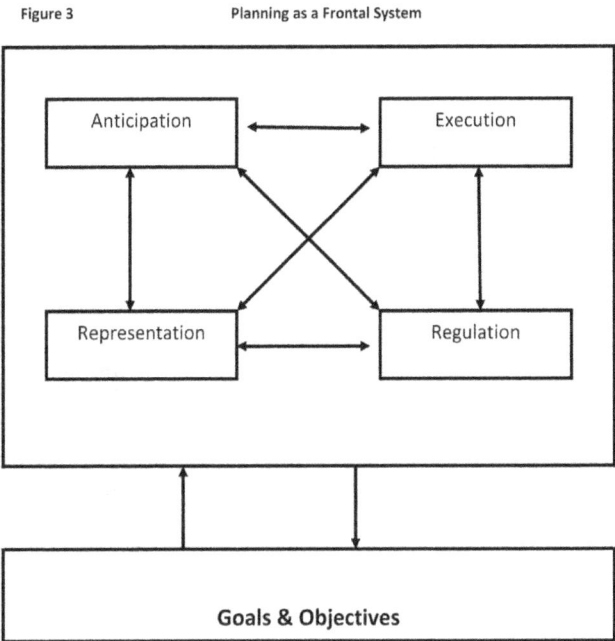

Notes on the Prefrontal Cortex

1. The prefrontal cortex (PFC) is the anterior part of the frontal lobes.
2. The PFC represents region in the front section of the frontal lobe. It is often divided into several regions such as the ventrolateral, dorsolateral, orbitofrontal, basal, orbital and frontopolar areas. The ventrolateral and dorsolateral regions are located on the side of these frontal lobes.
3. The ventrolateral prefrontal cortex (VLPFC) mediates some of the cognitive responses to negative emotion.
4. The two regions of the frontal lobes have generally distinct functions that relate to planning. Whereas the VLPFC is involved in promoting these aspects of the environmental stimuli that are consistent with goals of an individual, the DLPFC (Dorsolateral PFC) is mostly attentive to rules and reasoning as in problem solving. The first is named as the Ventral Affective System, in contrast to Dorsal Executive System.

Summary of Neural Correlates

1. The frontal lobes are the primary organs for EF and Planning. However, the DLPFC and its associated regions, such as anterior cingulate, ventrolateral, and ventromedial regions, appear to be helped by posterior regions of the cortex.
2. The main types of EF (Inhibition, Shifting, and Memory updates) indicate differential association. Initiating and sustaining a response rely on medial frontal region, task setting relies on left lateral region, and monitoring involved in checking and relies on right lateral regions.

Chapter 7

Decision-Making

It is not possible to provide a comprehensive account, of all of the actions of leaders, but to take some select examples, where some of the neuroscience is becoming available. The neuroscience of leadership is still in its infancy and so, we will use the results from studies of decision-making in other contexts to illustrate the possible neural systems that are at work within the leadership role. Knowing that it is possible to grow as a leader, we can begin to address some of the key ways in which leaders are challenged and to provide some understanding of how the brain works in these situations.

Two Systems for Decision Making

Decision-making is ubiquitous in our lives – we make conscious decisions many hundred times per day. Some of these decisions are relatively simple and involve no risk or uncertainty, like what to have for breakfast. But others are more complex, involve risks and can be emotionally laden, like who to hire and fire. An understanding of how such decisions are coded in the brain and what allows us to reach a decision can help us to justify our decisions.

However, much of our day-to-day decision making is made by our other-than-conscious (or unconscious) mind. The difference between conscious and other-than-conscious processing is not dependent on one area of the brain that is active when we are conscious and not active when we are not conscious of our actions. This implies that conscious and unconscious acts are based on activation in similar neural networks. There is no major qualitative difference between the types of information that our conscious and unconscious behaviours can access.

If the difference between the conscious and other than conscious mind does not lie in some particular activity within the brain, or in the type of information available to the two systems what must be different is the type of processing of information. This research has demonstrated that, on the whole conscious processes are slow, subject to reasoning or cost-benefit-analysis and more deliberate Daniel Kahneman (2011) refers to as slow thinking. In comparison, unconscious processing is fast, holistic and based on matching to previous patterns in order to draw conclusion: about potential actions based on past experience – fast thinking (Kahneman, 2011). Neither type of processing is superior, they are useful in particular situations and they can fail us in others.

In our society, there appears to be greater priority given to the slow, conscious system of decision-making. This is embedded in our school system. One reason that conscious processing might have been considered to be better than other than conscious processing is that there has been a tendency to equate conscious processing with rationality, while other-than conscious processing has been equated with being irrational. This is not the case.

Buying a house often involves other-than conscious process – know this is the house for me. Trying to explain why this is the case is often difficult. But this does not make the decision irrational. It probably means that you are matching to a huge catalogue of experiences with houses and comparing the new house with examples – both good and bad – very rapidly. In contrast, it is possible to work through a mathematical problem with absolute and conscious certainty that you are completing each step correctly – and still end up with the wrong answer.

The Neuroscience of Decision Making

Studies have shown that the neural decision-making processes that are used for conscious and other-than-conscious decision-making are very similar (Tobler, O'Doherty, Dolan & Schultz, 2007). When we make a decision, the brain determines what the expected value of a successful will be for this decision. The benefit or value of each outcome can be calculated. By assigning a value to each choice, the decision making process can compare between choices to see what provides the greatest benefit. *Neurons responsible for this coding have been found in the ventral striatum and prefrontal cortex* (Tobler et al, 2007).

Many decisions, however come with some risk. In this case, there has to be some neural calculation of the approximate expected, likelihood of each choice based on past experience. It might be that you calculate that one option has potentially high value, but if the likelihood that this outcome will occur is low, then this choice might be more risky than another choice with a lower value but a higher likelihood of success. *Neurons which code the uncertainty of value calculations have been found in the lateral orbito frontal crotex* (Tobler et al, 2007).

The choice made is dependent on not only the likelihood assigned to each decision, but also on the willingness of the individual to take risks. Some individuals are risk-seeking, while others are more risk-averse. Individuals who are risk-averse show greater activity to the amygdala, anterior insula, and anterior cingulate than individuals who are more risk-seeking. This suggests that risk-averse people have a high emotional response to risk.

It is therefore useful to be aware of whether individuals are more risk-averse or risk-seeking since then the bias in their reaction to risk can be taken into account.

Fast Decision-making

Humans are expert at detecting and understanding patterns of sensory information. These patterns are used to drive fast decision-making. The advantage of being very good pattern detectors, and thus using our fast thinking system to make decisions, is that we store behaviours that are appropriate responses to particular sensory patterns and so can make quick decisions about how to respond to these patterns when they appear in our environment. So, if we see a face, we might instantly decide whether it is friend or foe and therefore whether we want to approach or avoid the person. Sensory patterns drive behaviour – they are shortcuts (or heuristics) to our decision-making process.

Since fast decision-making process happen in milliseconds, it is possible to be completely unaware of the train of thought that has led to a particular decision. Most decisions will be based to some extent on trial and error and the accuracy of such decisions will be related to experience. The more that you make one type of decision, the more times you will have been able to assess the outcome. We remember which outcomes were positive and which we regretted. This provides more information on which to predict future outcomes, thus increasing the likely accuracy of prediction. As our experiences increase, we get better at making predictions. This drives greater use of the fast system. *Neurons that code information in decision-making are the same whether decision-making processes is conscious or unconscious, slow or fast.* Development of expertise leads to neuroplastic changes in the brain. An important part of the process of consolidating new ideas into memory takes place when we are not either focusing on current sensory input or retrieving long-term memories to make sense of sensory input. The time when our brains therefore have time to consolidate new information with the old is when we are sleeping. The importance of sleep to learning has now been established. While this might suggest that a good night's sleep is imperative for learning, it is important to appreciate the naps of 20-30 minutes during the day, timed to come immediately after a learning experience might be just – as effective as 8 hours of sleep overnight.

Acquisition of new expertise effects neural changes. For example, acquiring a new motor skill involves shifting motor representations within the parietal lobe from the associative cortex to sensorimotor cortex. Changes in the brain resulting from expertise in meditation involve increased activity across the prefrontal cortex, anterior cingulate cortex (ACC) and insula. This suggests that expertise in meditation increases awareness of visceral signal (insula), cognitive control (ACC) and self-regulation (prefrontal cortex).

Role of unconscious bias. Unconscious bias is a consequence of the fast decision-making processes. This represents a form of historical expertise that we have gained partly from our own experience, but also from the experience of our family, friends and society in general. One example of this might be that while we are not explicitly anti-religious, our families might have held these prejudices and so some of the language that is associated with these opinions can become embedded in our unconscious. You might find yourself repeating something that you would have heard your parents often say, despite it not fitting your own beliefs and values. These phrases, and the opinions that drive them, can then become apparent in our unconscious actions, whereas we would never express them consciously.

Biases of the fast thinking system. There are many shortcuts (heuristics) that drive behaviour. Kahneman (2011) has researched a large number of these biases and provide description. A representative sample of such shortcuts can be presented here.

1. Confirmation bias: It denotes that propensity to seek information that confirms our opinions and, thus, to ignore that goes against them. Clearly this bias has a downside in that we can then act on partial information instead of being prepared to include options from both sides of an argument. However, this has a benefit, since our beliefs and values form an integral part of our sense of self (ventromedial prefrontal cortex), confirming our opinions is a means to confirm our sense of self.

2. Negativity bias: It refers to the tendency of paying greater attention to negative than positive events. This is problematic since it can lead to behaviour that is more risk-averse than realistically required. However, again, this bias in our thinking provides an advantage. By paying attention to negative evens, we are able to take action to prevent bad things (survival value).

3. Availability bias: This bias can cause all kinds of

distortions in the way we estimate probability. For example, a high profile bankruptcy will increase our estimation of the probability of business failure.

4. Affect bias: Affect heuristic is a term psychologists use to describe how emotions shape our most fundamental views of the world and out attitudes. Our immediate emotional response to a stimulus, for example seeing a face, colours our perception of the person, without being examined or challenged. It is not surprising, as the role of emotion in our brain is to tell us what to approach and what to avoid.

There are other heuristics. These are experience-based processes for solving problems often relying on trial and error. The term is used for unconscious, instinctive or learned processes which are quick, but can lead to mistakes.

Slow Thinking

Slow thinking can be equated with reasoning through a problem consciously in order to evaluate and compare all of the available options. This requires that a value, and the risk associated with each option, is calculated. For example, when deciding whether to change a job, the value of the current job and the risk associated with keeping it might be compared with the value associated with a new job and the risk of obtaining that position. This contrasts to fast thinking which is equated to emotional decision-making or "gut-feeling".

In line with these two decision-making processes, there are different processing systems in the brain that are activated when we think with our head versus thinking with our gut. The ventromedial prefrontal cortex has been in emotional reasoning (Damasio, 1996) while the lateral and dorsolateral prefrontal cortex is implicated in reasoning and logic. The brain areas used during logical processing have been assessed using logical reasoning task where participants have to determine whether sets of statement are logically valid or invalid. For example:

A.   No reptiles can grow hair
       Some elephants can grow hair
       No elephants are reptiles

B.   All gossip rags are popular
       All hello magazines are gossip rags
       All hello magazines are popular

Tests of this nature activate the lateral and dorsolateral prefrontal cortex. This area of the brain is also activated during tasks involving planning and design, cognitive dissonance, and inhibition (Goel & Dolan, 2003). Clearly we have evolved a neural system that is able to help us work through cognitive, non-emotional problems at conscious level.

However, we often have to think logically about situations that are emotionally charged. What happens in the brain? Goel and Dolan (2003) tested this by comparing responses to non-emotional logical problems to those when the problems were emotionally charged. For example,

All handicapped are capable
All amputees are handicapped
Some amputees are not capable

These stimuli were found to produce an emotional response as they were being solved. In this case, the ventromedial precortex was activated. Interestingly, both the accuracy with which participants correctly answered the problems and the speed of problem solving were found to be same for both sets of problems. Additionally, activation of the two reasoning systems was reciprocal-activating dorsolateral prefrontal cortex reduced the activation in ventromedial prefrontal cortex and vice versa. This suggests that we have two systems for thinking through logical reasoning problems – one for cold, non-emotional content and the other for emotionally laden content.

Slow logical thinking is pervasive in our day-to-day life. We use it all the time. This is reflected in the number of different neural systems that can be called upon for this type of thinking. Thus, different neural networks have been shown to be active when we use inductive and deductive reasoning (Goel & Dolan, 2004), or when solve abstract mathematical problems versus similar problems with concrete examples. Additionally, the right lateral prefrontal cortex is activated when propositions are logically valid but the premise is not believed (Goel & Dolan, 2003).

These systems would be sufficient to guarantee that we could think through problems accurately, coming to the right conclusion each time. However, there is some suggestion that consciously thinking through choices too much can impair decision-making. In addition, our conscious thinking processes are prone to biases.

Decision-making in Complex Environment

There are certain elements which complicate the decision-making process. In one study participants were given a commodity and were asked to state its selling price. In another session they were asked to state its buying price. The finding of a ratio of 2:1 between selling and buying price has been replicated in many studies.

Another way in which slow decision-making is not

rational is that the value of objects does not remain constant over time. Research demonstrates that rewards in future are less valued than those in the present (a cause for procrastination).

Third, the degree of stress affects decision making. Stress results in a blunting of the response to future reward in the medial prefrontal cortex. This can decrease the flexibility of decision-making since reward of a novel decision is lower, and thus can increase the activation of habitual responding.

In the real world, decisions are made when there is considerable uncertainties about possible outcomes. In some cases, both the value of the outcome and the degree of risk are known. A more difficult decision-making scenario arises when the value of the outcome is known but the risk cannot be calculated. The degree of ambiguity involved in a decision appears to be coded in the orbitofrontal cortex and/or insula. Thus, the decision-making processes that we activate when faced with missing information depend crucially on our tolerance for ambiguity.

Decision-making Fatigue

Our decision making capacity is like a battery which is successively drained a little by each decision we take. Eventually, over the course of a day, the battery will flatten and our ability to make difficult decisions will be depleted. This is referred to as ego depletion because it is the decision-making part of yourself (your ego) that is being depleted.

Decision fatigue can have important consequences for decision-making. This can impair ability to trust others. Additionally, leaders will exert self-regulation to work through decision fatigue, but this takes a high toll such that they are unable to address important decisions that arise after this depletion. Thus, using decision resources wisely can prevent a situation where a leader no longer has sufficient decision-making power when this is required unexpectedly.

It is important to top up your battery using a number of different tips and tricks

1   **Sleep will revitalize your battery – even short naps will work.**

2   **Add energy through glucose – your decision-making battery is depleted by lack of food.**

3   **Feeling more energetic will increase your battery life.**

4   **Feeling motivated and believing that there is no limit to your capacity for will power will increase your battery life.**

5   **Giving great feedback (constructive or positive) will increase other people's battery life.**

Chapter 8

Changing Self and Others

A great deal of the work of a leader involves change – in their own and others' performance, behaviours, skills and attitudes. Our brain is changing all the time; every new stimulus or thought creates some new connections; familiar stimuli and thinking reinforce existing connections and every mental and physical action is the result of activating new or existing networks of connections between neurons.

However, in order for someone to change their physical or mental behaviours sustainably (to create new habits), their brain needs to create new and robust connections between neurons. We also know that the adult brain remains plastic (i.e., changeable) throughout life and that its connections can be changed by learning and practice.

Habitual Behaviours

As adults, most of what we do on daily basis, how we react to familiar stimuli and effect regular goal, is habitual and automatic. Experience shapes and patterns of behaviour through which we normally achieve our daily goals, walking downstairs, eating breakfast, typing on our computers. If it works reasonably efficiently we do not need to consciously plan how to walk. In contrast, a toddler has to work out how to get down from a chair and get into mother's lap.

Such habitual behaviour is the result of many years of learning and practice. It is the result of neural networks being reinforced through repeated use to the point where their activation is the easiest option for achieving certain goals in certain contexts. A useful analogy is like the deepest of several connected channels running down a hill. Water will find its way there by itself. Goals do not have to be conscious in order to trigger habitual behaviours. A student who has the long-standing habit of coming to his/her study room after classroom activities would start working in the study room automatically.

New behaviours take time and conscious effort to learn. *Learning can be described as the forging of new connections.* Once forged and successfully repeated over a significant period of time, their connections become the deepest channel, the default path for signals in the brain. It is now believed that the neural pattern may physically be created in the brain.

Think about your own deeply engrained habit. Not just those like eating and travelling but some of the small things you do every day or every week. For example, how do you normally react to an interception – with a smile or a frown? How do you start your management team meeting? Do you go straight to the point you make or you encourage others to give a range of inputs? It can take months or years to create habitual mental and physical behaviours. Changing these involves the creation of new pathways, which with use over time become the easier, default routes for neural signals to travel. The old connections, if not used, are gradually puned.

> ### A Case
> Manna, a very bright and able colleague, who managed the IT system providing customer information and support for a large services organization, was known as difficult because she had the habit of starting most responses with the word no. This had served her well in the past, when she was the junior receiving orders and requests from everywhere, as it gave her time think and plan, but as the leader some 200 sales, clerical and IT staff it was a significant disadvantage. A mentor helped her see the need for change and she worked hard at becoming more approachable.

Changing Brain

A number of factors are needed to change brain so that it enables new patterns of mental or physical behaviours. The first is **focused attention.** Although adult brains continue to be plastic, and we have some 86 billion neurons capable of roughly one million billion connections, we do not have infinite capacity. Our brain is a competitive environment in which different paths compete for resources. These resources can be chemical, such as the oxygen and glucose that are required for energy, and hormones which trigger particular effects, and physical, such as the limited capacity of our working memory which can hold only some five to nine items at one time, and the speed at which a signal can pass across a number of neural connections.

Some people might say the brain is inherently lazy. In other words, the brain chooses the most energy efficient path. We know that the higher order brain functions, anything complex involving working memory and prefrontal cortex

(PFC), such as conscious processing of inputs, conscious decision making, complex concepts, planning strategizing, self-reflection, regulating our emotions and channelizing energy from them, are very energy intensive.

Attention appears to be this mechanism by which these limited resources are focused on a particular stimulus, physical activity or mental task. Attention allows for new neural connections to be forged and progressively strengthened. The old unused ones are gradually pruned. *The pruning of neural connections happens throughout life, but there are two periods when it is most intensive and causes massive changes around the age of two and adolescence. It is the reason teenagers need so much sleep and fuel, and underlies changes in their personalities and moods.*

It appears that focused attention is needed for significant changes in the brain. But for leaders, focusing is not enough. The leaders must have the capacity to shift attention when necessary.

The new connections are sustained and embedded through the second factor, deliberate **practice or repetition.** Forming a new network or pathway of multiple connections (or mental map), is not enough, as a new connection is fragile. For it to remain usable, it needs to be used again and again until it is well established. *"Use it or lose it" is indeed a critical principle.* Re-using a set of connection, such as those created as result of learning a new skill like driving a car not only improves that skill but gradually changes the location of that map in the brain, so that it needs less conscious attention and hence fewer resources and efforts to accomplish. This explains the difference between a skilled driver and a novice one. It has been observed that cab drivers' mid posterior hippocampus starts reducing its size in retirement after a relatively short period.

Underlying focused attention and practice is the need for the **motivation, will power or self-control** to change. Without this, focusing attention and practicing will not be sustained enough to deliver the long-term robustness of new connections that are acquired for long change. Finally, the **environment** has to be conducive to focusing attention. In situations of danger and uncertainty the brain's resources are driven by the overwhelming need for survival. The need focuses attention on the source of danger and on trying to predict where the next threat will appear, on escape or full frontal battle rather than an innovative or creative solution. The most important part of our environment is other people and our relationship with them.

Further Explication of Factors

Focused attention. Focused attention is driven both "bottom-up" and "top-down" systems (i.e., by external stimuli that we do not control, or by our goals and will). Our attention is focused involuntarily on "bottom-up" stimuli that are most relevant to us, either through genetically programmed behaviour, social significance, and so on. For example, when we perceive an immediate threat, such as a car that is veering towards us at speed, our attention is focused.

Attention is voluntarily focused, "top-down" in service to our conscious goals. For example, when we want to do something that is of interest (like hitting a tennis ball), top-down attention is focused. Top-down attention can also be focused by non-conscious goals.

The presence of focused attention determines a significant change in brain structure (Merzenich & associates). Although receiving and processing a stimulus creates changes in adults, these are less lasting than those created by deliberate attention. It is also possible that focused attention is necessary for the capture of explicit memory (semantic and episodic).

The ability to focus attention can be improved through practice. There is non considerable evidence that mindfulness meditation is one of practicing that does just that.

Repetition and practice. The effect of practice can be explained at neuronal level by the *"Hebbian principle of cells that fire together wire together"*. Repeated firing of neurons at the same time strengthens their connections and increases the speed and efficiency of the linked networks. Linked firing is also thought to be involved in the creation of memories. The corollary is that neurons that fire together only once, or only a couple of times, have fragile links to each other, unless the experience is highly emotionally charged.

Repetition and practice works not just for the motor cortex, but for sensory and cognitive activity. Practice needs to be sustained over a significant period of time. Depending on the activity, various experiments have derived required period. Klinberg describes an experiment in which it took five weeks of cognitive training to change patterns of activity in the frontal and parietal lobes. An experiment in 1995, by Pascual Leone, with some participants practicing on keyboards and a control group just thinking about the same movements, demonstrated that both groups changed the relevant motor cortex area. Mental, as well as physical, practice change the structure of the brain.

This has the most prefound significance for leaders who are grappling with significant organizational changes. It cannot happen overnight. Changing self and other needs time.

Motivation, will power and self-control. It is important to recognize that motivation, will power, and self-control are closely interconnected. These factors need to be harnessed to achieve significant, sustainable behaviour and attitude change towards a consciously set goal.

Human are motivated. They are motivated to act in terms of responses towards external and internal stimuli. This can be both conscious and non-conscious.

Whether or not humans have free will is still hotly debated. In 1999 Benjamin Libet established that some 100-200 milliseconds before a conscious decision to move a finger, for example, a readiness potential was measurable in that part of the brain that controls that finger movement. Libet concluded that our non-conscious mind had made the decision before our conscious mind was aware of it – hence no free will. But he maintained that our conscious mind had about 150 milliseconds to choose between allowing and countermanding that decision. These findings are still controversial. The meaning of the readiness potential has been disputed. They may however explain why exercising will and making decisions are such hard work.

That human will or will power (determination to pursue a chosen goal or action) exists has been demonstrated by experiments. Roy Baumeister is a leading researcher. A key manifestation of will power is self-control or self-management, the ability to resist impulsive desires. Exercising self-control appears to correlate with increased activity in the right ventrolateral prefrontal cortex (RVLPFC). According to Baumeister, will power like a muscle, can be trained through repeated practice.

In order to change behaviour to achieve a goal, exercising will or self-control to keep attention focused on the goal and on the changes needed would seem a key part of the top-down process. Will is also essential to persistence in practicing until the change is successfully embedded and routinized. Once routinized, the bottom-up system plays its role.

Motivation and will can thus be seen as parts of the brain's mechanism for bottom-up and top-down focusing of attention on what is most important and relevant and enabling self-control towards the achievement of goals.

Environment. A leader has the seminal role of creating environments which make it easier for people to achieve organizational goals. These are indeed leaders who recognize that it is easier to work with the grain of the brain than against it. Having recognized the paramount importance of focused attention to enable change, of emotions for motivation and the need for practice over significant periods of time, they are more likely to create environments in which individuals and teams can change themselves and each other. Such environments will have reduced distractions, they will have many opportunities for the corporate goals to be clearly articulated and repeated, and the goals will be few and coherent, not conflicting.

Having explicit goals appears to create motivation. There is some evidence that writing them down not only helps clarify them but also increases the chances that we will achieve them.

Actions and Reflections
- Use the power of goals to trigger focused attention
- Anything that supports practice is useful (getting self-help groups to do role plays)
- Engage in mindful meditation, even for a few minutes a day before important calls or meeting
- Set an example of how to avoid unnecessary

distractions and offer training how to avoid them (time-management). Discourage multi-tasking.

- Provide a varied and appropriate mix of incentives, which, with feedback are closely linked with desired outcomes
- Finally, where appropriate, allow people to have sufficient time to develop expertise. Frequent changes can get in the way of performance when in-depth domain knowledge is needed.

Chapter 9

Emotional Styles

Abstract

The cognitive revolution in the early part of the twentieth century had posited a picture of incompatibility between cognition and emotion. However, the advent of neuroscience and the use of sophisticated technology of brain research has changed the scenario. The paper presents and defends the proposition that the process of balancing the feeling and logic is essential for effective decision making. Important cases are cited and emotional styles are explicated. The mood map is also presented. Suggestions are outlined in terms brain-adaptive management of emotional styles and moods for living a fulfilled life.

There has been a major representation of human nature. The advent of science and Renaissance-inspired thinking after the middle ages have proclaimed cognitive processes as the pinnacle of human experience, relegating emotions to animalistic states. Bashing emotions out of mental processes ensured objective thinking "Stay cool", "don't be emotional", "you are over-reacting" and other phrases like these showcase the aggressive and hostile attitude towards emotion from our modern societies. The main message was: *The less the emotion, the better the decision.* But can humans live, think and act without emotions? Are emotions evolutionary leftovers that diminish our rational thinking? Should we try to suppress them to become better decision makers. Neuroscience and psychology answer these questions with a big No.

Two Illustrative Cases

In 1848, Phineas Gage, a 25-year old construction foreman for the Rutland and Burlington Railroad (USA), was the victim of a tragic accident. In order to lay new tracks, the terrain had to be leveled, and Gage was in charge of blasting. His task involved drilling holes in the rock, pouring some gunpowder in each hole, covering it with sand, and tamping the material down with a large tamping iron before detonating it with a fuse. On the fateful day, the gunpowder exploded while Gage was tamping it, launching the 3-cm thick, 90-cm-long tamping iron through his face, skull, and brain and out the other side.

Amazingly Gage survived his accident, but he survived it a changed man. Before accident, Gage gad been a responsible, intelligent, and socially well-adapted man, who was liked by his friends and fellow workers. Once recovered, he appeared to be as able-bodied and intellectually capable as before, but his personality and emotional life had totally changed. Formerly a religious, respectful, reliable man, Gage became irreverent and impulsive. In particular, his abundant profanity offended many. He became so unreliable and undependable that he soon lost his job and was never again able to hold a responsible position.

Gage became an itinerant, roaming the country for a dozen years until his death in San Francisco. His bizarre accident and apparently successful recovery made headlines around the world, but his death went largely unnoticed. Five years later, neurologist John Harlow was granted permission from Gage's family to exhume the body. Since then, Gage's skull and the tamping iron have been on display in the Warren Anatomical Medical Museum at Harvard University.

In 1994, Damasio and her colleagues brought the power of computerized reconstruction to bear on Gage's case. They began by taking an X-ay of the skull and measuring it precisely, paying particular attention to the position of the entry and exit holes. From the measurements, they reconstructed the accident and determined the likely region of gage's brain damage. It was apparent that the damage to Gage's brain affected both *medical prefrontal lobes,* which we know are involved in planning and emotion.

Another interesting observation pertains to the case of Elliot (Damasio, 2008). Elliot was diagnosed with a fast-growing tumour in the middle area of his brain, which was pushing both frontal lobes upwards. Following successful surgery to remove it, Elliot emerged healthy but changed. Although he was able to think logically and calculate decisions rationally his actual behaviour was antisocial and far from normal. This change led to monumental insights into the role of emotions in decision making and overall in a healthy human life. In a nutshell, it revealed that emotions are at least as important as any other brain function in the way we take decisions and act on them. Decisions without emotion are not just wrong but they may also be dangerous.

Damasio (2004), a renowned neuroscientist and neurobiologist, makes a startling statement in his book *Descartes' Error*: Reduction in emotion may constitute an equally source of irrational behaviour. He convincingly claimed that when emotion is absent there is a counter-intuitive connection with distorted behaviour, which reveals the sophisticated but strong dependence of vigorous reasoning on healthy emotions.

The Role of Emotion

The remarkable insight in Gage's and Elliot cases is that while their high level cognitive functions were intact after the surgery, their decision making and behaviour were leading to long-term isolation from the people around them. When subjected to tests on perceptual ability, past memory, short-term memory, new learning, language, arithmetic, motor skills Elliot performed exceptionally. He appeared to be a totally normal person ready to perform his daily personal and professional tasks as everybody else. But his actual behaviour was catastrophic for both. How can somebody pass all those tests, appear totally logical but perform so badly socially and personally? Yet this is a phenomenon that neuroscience confirms again and again (Miller et al, 2008). The ability to use emotions in decision making and behaviour is as important as, and sometimes more important than, the ability to use logic. Evolutionarily speaking, emotions developed much earlier in our long history and played a crucial role in making choices. The executive brain, as the latest addition to our skill, depends greatly on emotions to drive and direct its decisions. Elliot, Phineas Gage and other cases in medical history had actually damaged their neurological paths that inject emotions into their choices and this led to long-term disastrous behaviours. Switching off your emotional brain when taking managerial and business decisions is not only neurologically impossible it is also very dangerous thing to do.

The biggest impact of emotion in decision making is morality. This is the ability to weigh a decision in its later stages based on the possible impact on ourselves and others. It is close to empathy since it helps us share the feeling that an action can cause. People with damaged emotional neural pathways (amygdala-limbic system and hypothalamus – sympathetic response) cannot use their moral compass to guide their decision making processes and behaviour and thus end up making wrong choices both for themselves and others. Actually, there are two medical terms for people who do not have the ability to use empathy and thus take only cold-blooded decisions that eventually work against them and society: psychopaths and sociopaths. Jon Ronson (2011), in his well-known book *The Psychopath Test: A journey through the madness industry* and before him Paul Babiak and Robert Hare (2006) in their famous book *Snakes in Suits: When psychopaths go to work,* argue that reliable characteristics of a psychopath are absence of empathy, remorse, and loving kindness. Amazingly enough these are the elements that traditionally schools, MBA programmes and companies tried to push out of future professionals and executives trying to boost their cold-blooded, calculative reasoning. Are we trying to make psychopaths out of managers, leaders and people in general? *Modern leaders need to move away from such archaic mindsets and be aware of neuroscience-based realities about what make us great in companies and life.*

Apart from enhancing our decision making, emotions are significant for leadership because they are the bases of motivation. The Latin root of the English word emotion is "to move" and this is in plain sight since the word itself includes the term 'enhancing motion'. Elaine Fox (2013) has elaborated two basic brain systems: Amygdala as the fear / emergency / avoidance / pessimism centre and nucleus accumbens as the pleasure / excitement / acceptance / optimism centre. These two centres drive must of us away from or closer to situations.

Emotions run our brain. They are usually classified into three categories. First, the fleeting emotions we feel in any given moment. Second, the traits, which are emotions that have long-term presence. Third, the moods that are somewhere between these two. Neurologically speaking, emotional styles are closer to our understanding how brain wiring affects our emotions and we will start our emotional journey with them.

Emotional Styles

The advent of neuroscience and the accompanying technology allow us to peer into the brain to observe how neurons fire and connect with each other. Richard Davidson, famous for his research on Tibetan monks' brains, has developed a specific categorization of emotional styles (Davidson & Begley, 2012). Emotional styles are much closer to underlying brain systems than emotional states and traits. Davidson considers these styles as atoms of our emotional life – fundamental building blocks.

Davidson established *six* emotion styles. Each style lies on a continuum with two extremes on its sides.

Style 1: Resilience. On one extreme, the style is fast recovery from adversity and, on the other slow recovery. In essence the style determines the way we respond to a negative event. If you cannot recover easily from a setback and you keep dwelling on negative emotions, then you are closer to the slow recovery extreme. These two extremes depend on the interplay between the amygdala and prefrontal cortex. The more the amygdala is activated over the prefrontal cortex, the more in the slow recovery extreme you will be. The more the prefrontal cortex is activated over the amygdala, the faster you will recover. Leaders need to move quickly away from disappointments and consider new alternatives with high energy almost daily. Students and organization clients to look fast for lessons learned, new alternatives, and reasons to be active as soon as a setback appears.

Style 2: Outlook. This is the popular pessimism-optimism continuum. Elaine Fox (2013) speaks of *rainy and sunny brain.* Outlook denotes the way we view everyday events. Do we tend to search for the negative side of every situation or do we always look on the bright side? The interplay of the left frontal cortex and the nucleus accumbens, our pleasure centre, is in focus here. The more signals go from the prefrontal cortex to the nucleus accumbens, gearing it towards increased activity, the more you are on the positive extreme.

Our pleasure centre operates mainly under dopamine and opiates, and these two are responsible for different pleasure outcomes. Dopamine activity is associated with anticipation and opiates with pleasure. This means that leaders need to manage those two pleasure states differently. The feeling of excitement coming from anticipating a result, an event, a meeting, a presentation, is not based on the same chemicals. Dopamine is involved in the first and opiates in the second (different mechanisms for anticipatory and achievement emotions).

Style 3: Social intuition. Effectively reading the

intentions and emotions of others is essential for great leadership as no one can inspire others while being oblivious to their states of mind. On the one extreme of this continuum is a socially confused person and on the other is a socially intuitive person. When our sensitivity to other people's emotions is heightened, we have the basis of *empathy* and *compassion*. The amygdala is also at play here but this time together with the fusiform gyrus. The fusiform gyrus is located on the temporal and occipital lobes of our cortex and it has been associated with various forms of recognition. A study by Josef Parvizi and his associates (2012) in the Stanford School of Medicine identified this brain region for face recognition. When the amygdala is activated more than the fusiform gyrus when looking at people's faces, it is a strong indication of a confused style. When the opposite happens, this indicates a highly socially intuitive person. Dr. Paul Ekman's (2007) pioneering work on studying human facial expression all around the world has revealed the evolutionary role of our ability to tell other people's emotional state by observing their faces. Early in our development as a species, when our capacity for language was still limited, we depended on reading people's faces fast and in a subconscious way to adjust our behaviour and increase our chances of survival.

To improve on this continuum, we need to work both on quieting the amygdala, fighting its hijacking potential and trying to become better in reading other people's emotional cues on their face, bodily movements, voices and actions. Observing your friends and close colleagues for emotional cues and discussing with them their emotional state by giving your evaluation is a good start.

Style 4: Self-awareness. The main brain region

responsible for this awareness is the *insula,* or *insular cortex,* which is part of our cerebral cortex. This is because the insula contains a map of brain organs, receiving and sending signals to them. The higher the activity in the insula, the better the self-awareness. The lower the activity in the insula, the worse the conscious experience and understanding of our own emotions. The famous ancient phrase "know Thyself" is the essence of the self-awareness continuum. At one extreme, our ability of introspection is very weak, severing the connection between our inner self and our conscious self. At the other extreme we can be very sensitive to our internal changes and signals. Taking time to quietly, and in isolation, assess your bodily signals when feeling excited, positively or negatively, can be crucial for understanding your emotional state accurately and acting accordingly.

Style 5: Context sensitivity. On one extreme on this continuum is people tuned in to the environment and in other, tuned out. Tuned in means emotional synchronization while tuned out means emotional disconnection with a situation. For example, managers sometimes make jokes in a crucial moment of a presentation, or become over serious when a business partner is trying rightfully to lighten up a conversation. The brain region associated with such emotional synchronization is the hippocampus. It has a key role in memory formation, but it plays a vital role in fitting or tuning behaviours to contexts or situations. A weaker, or even a smaller, hippocampus can mean complete inappropriate emotions and subsequent behaviour. Furthermore, contextual learning is diminished in such cases. Thus we need to make sure that our internal state and external requirements fit both in order to behave accordingly.

Some of the recommendations involve: taking time for the description of the situation, taking time for the description of reactions of self and others, internal listening, external listening, and constant listening.

Style 6: Attention. One extreme of this dimension is a focused person while on the other extreme is an unfocused one. Do you have trouble focusing on the person talking to you from across the meeting table? Do you feel your mind wandering every time you look at the detailed monthly reports of your organization? The prefrontal cortex, or executive brain, is responsible for focus since higher activity can produce a condition called 'phased locking' which is the ultimate focus. In this condition the engagement of the prefrontal cortex is perfectly timed with the external stimulus, meaning that you are mentally in line with what you are paying attention to. Being *laser-focused* (Buhayar, 2013) on execution, growth, new products and market opportunities is an important ingredient in leadership tool-box.

However, too much focus is not always an advantage. Gallate and his associates (2012) revealed that creative people benefit the most when taking a break from focusing on a given problem and that this process allows for non-conscious processes to take over and provide insightful solution. *Too much focus inhibits creativity, but lose* focus inhibits performance and productivity. At the same time, there are situations when extreme focus is needed, such as in certain negotiations, and thus the intensity of focus has to be determined on a case-by-case basis.

Mood Patterns

The long-term effects of emotional styles on how we

think and behave resemble the long-term effects of personality. They follow us through a large part of our lives. They can change to better fit our leadership challenges but this takes time and much targeted efforts. In a more short-term horizon, our emotions are highly influenced by our moods. Modern leaders need to be aware and try to control them since they form the fertile ground for our everyday emotional reactions.

Dr. Liz Miller (2009), a leading expert on moods, has the following observation:

We all have moods all the time …… Moods are an internal measure of how we are. We do not express our moods directly. Instead we express them indirectly in the way we think, communicate, behave and see the world. …… Almost all our anger reflects an underlying irritable, anxious mood. This mood has provided the soil that allowed the emotion of anger to grow.

It is our general mood that will determine greatly the type of emotions we will express at any given moment. Thus, by getting into the right mood and avoiding counterproductive ones, we can reach for the right set of emotions in any situation and use them to further our leadership skills.

Nurturing a positive mood is integral to concentration and clear thinking. In a particularly interesting study, Raby Nadler of the Western University of Canada and her colleagues (2010) have demonstrated that people in a positive mood outperform those in neutral or negative moods. Those in positive mood show cognitive flexibility and make a greater use of their prefrontal cortex, our executive brain.

Miller's (2009) now famous categorization of moods uses two variables to plot a **mood map**: energy on the one axis and well-being on the other.

Mood Map

	Negative	Well-being	Positive
High	**The panic mood** tension, fear irritation frustration jumpy attitude		**The rocket mood** strongly motivated highly pleased fast moving smile on face
Low			
	The downer mood mentally exhausted often sad cannot hide boredom physically fatigued		**The guru mood** calm highly content satisfied create stability

(Energy)

A leader does not have to be at these extremes though to identify his or her moods as the *Rocket,* the *Guru,* the *Downer* or the *Panic.* Even milder versions capture the essence of each category. Keeping yourself on the positive side and increasingly on the high energy side is of paramount importance since even solving difficult math problems and speaking in public are associated with appraising your feelings as excitement instead of anxiety. Alison Wood Brooks (2013) from Harvard Business School found that when there is emotional arousal because of an upcoming challenge, people do much better when they interpret this as excitement than anxiety. A positive rocket mood helps you to do exactly that. However, there are also occasions when low-intensity moods such as interest and calmness are helpful.

A great challenge for well-lived life and effective leadership is to move from moods to great feelings. In such a context, the role of emotional intelligence can hardly be underestimated (Goleman, 1995). Brain without emotions is a malfunctioning brain and this is something that organizations, leaders, managers and people have to understand quickly in order to calibrate better towards a brain-based lifestyle. Emotions help us think faster and with morality, move ourselves and others and boost our cognitive capacity for advanced performance. Being aware of our emotional styles and moods, and applying a holistic approach that takes into account both the internal and external worlds, can help us bypass the outdated notion of incompatibility of emotion and cognition.

Chapter 10

Emotional Management

Simplistic views of management in organizations are dominating management styles, primarily because the neurobiological basis of emotion is missing from basic, and even from advanced management education and training. In other words, the majority of management education programmes around the world are based on principles and practices supported by the traditional jargon of management science neglecting critical findings of neuroscience that call for emotional and social intelligence to become integral skills in management and leadership. What emotions do we have and how can leaders acknowledge them within themselves and others in their organizations? Emotions produce tremendous moving powers and modern leaders can no longer be oblivious of how they actually work and of the combinations that can work better for them in their organizations.

The Basic Emotions in the Brain

There is a wider consensus that emotions are necessary for human motivation and action. Without emotions there is no urgency to behave in any way, to transfer from a stable conditions of homeostasis ('standing still') to a more dynamic conditions of movement. So the higher the need for change, the more urgent the need for emotion to keep people changing. The brain is actually built for that, but are we using it appropriately?

The emotional state in the brain is often described as a continuum, with positive and negative on the two extremes, and neutral in the middle. Both extremes are there to make us move, either towards or away from an object, a person or a situation. Fox (2013) describes these two conditions as the approach/avoidance systems in our brain. The number of emotions that exist form the toolbox for leaders to use for themselves and others to activate the avoid/approach systems.

In the beginning terms are to be distinguished. Emotional states (emotions are distinguished from their subjective perceptions (feelings); their midterm patterns are "moods" and their long-term, personality-like (trait-like) models ae emotional styles.

Although we use various names to describe our internal states, scientists discovered that there is actually only a small number that dominate our brains and bodies. Both Ekman and his teacher Tomkins studied facial expressions to reveal *basic human emotions.* Ekman's (2007) model of universal facial expressions found that, all around the world, six basic emotions do exist: *anger, disgust, fear, happiness, sadness* and *surprise.* Tomkins' model provide a list of nine basic emotions or "affects", some in high/low pairs. Nathanson (1992) claims that these emotions are "hard-wired, preprogrammed, genetically transmitted mechanisms that exist in each of us.

Tomkins' model include the following:
1. Enjoyment (low) / Joy (high)
2. Interest (low) / Excitement (high)
3. Surprise (low) / Startle (high)

4.   Anger (low) / Rage (high)
5.   Distress (low) / Anguish (high)
6.   Fear (low) / Terror (high)
7.   Shame (low) / Humiliation (high)
8.   Disgust (Negative reaction to bad offering)
9.   Dissmell (Negative reaction to repelling situation)

The latest research on Ekman's model reduces the number of basic emotions on facial expressions down to just four: happiness, sadness, fear/surprise, anger/disgust (Jack et al, 2014). Both Ekman's and Tomkins' models have influenced both scientific and non-scientific professionals around the world, mainly because of their straight forwardness and direct relation to the human face. These sets of basic emotions involve both macro and micro-expressions of the face. Since micro-expressions are not consciously manipulated, they are presumed to reveal deeper brain structures.

Lovhelm (2012) offers a comprehensive link to chemicals in the brain. The model specifies the role of three monoamine neurotransmitting chemicals in the brain: serotonin, dopamine, noradrenaline.

- Serotonin (a chemical related to being able to control behaviour, think clearly, regulate mood, avoid aggression): high in positive emotions of joy and excitement as well as in surprise disgust.

- Dopamine (arousal hormone that gets us ready for action through anticipating results): high in positive emotions of joy and excitement but also in the negative pair fear/terror and anger/rage.

- Noradrenaline (stress hormone, also known as norepinephrine): high on distress, anger, interest, and surprise, an interesting mix of positive, negative and neutral ones.

Regardless of the model of emotion, leaders and managers need to understand the basic emotions and separate them from feelings, moods and styles in order to be able to work with them more effectively in various challenges. Being aware of the automatic reactions emotions have on behaviour, leaders can better steer their actions and the actions of others. *The oversimplified and sometimes offensive model of the carrot and stick approach as a caricature representation of the avoid/approach systems in the brain has to be urgently replaced by a more realistic and complex knowledge of emotions and how they actually affect our motivation.*

Going Beyond the Basic Emotions (Dr. Plutchik's Combination)

Understanding and dealing effectively with core emotions are the first necessary step for becoming a better leader. The next, and more advanced step, is to understand how emotions are combined in order to create the wealth of feelings we experience in everyday life. In this direction, Dr. Robert Plutchik, in the beginning of the 1980s, went beyond the identification of basic emotions. He suggested that each emotion, when combined with others, produces new ones and that each one forms the opposite of another emotion. By studying Dr. Plutchik's combinations we get a more complex but also a more representative view of the functions of emotions in ourselves and others.

Dr. Plutchik (2001) suggested that each of his eight core emotions has an opposite one: joy has sadness, trust has disgust, fear has anger, and surprise has anticipation. Knowing the opposite of an emotion is important, because the moment you experience a basic emotion, you can tell which one is on the other side and take necessary action.

For example, when you do not trust a colleague and you want to improve the situation, you need to lower disgust. The same goes for surprise and anticipation. Fast-moving changes in organizations and the huge impact of complexity in our working lives has made anticipation a difficult emotion to sustain. Constant anticipation can lead to certainty and certainty means security and control. Since these are in short supply on modern business environments, if we do not want ourselves and our people to be constantly surprised (an emotion that can easily develop into a negative one) then we should do our best to minimize creating rigid anticipation for specific outcomes as a precondition of well-being, personally and collectively. The small / purposive bets approach can be very useful in avoiding big certainties and rigid anticipations. A strong sense of purpose can also help develop healthy an open anticipation and thus mitigate constant unpleasant surprise.

Dr. Plutchik goes further in suggesting two-emotion combinations. Knowing the ingredients can help us deal with bester.

- Joy and trust create love (A). the opposite is remorse (B), created by sadness and disgust.
- Trust and fear create submission (C), the opposite is contempt (D), created by disgust and anger.
- Fear and surprise create awe (E). The opposite is aggressiveness (F), created by anger and anticipation.
- Surprise and sadness create disapproval (G). The opposite is created by optimism (H), created by anticipation and joy.

A scary boss who brings results usually leads through submission and fear. Regardless of the advantages of obedience, it can lead to immoral actions as exemplified by Milgram's (1974) experiment on obedience and Zimbardo's

(2007) prison experiment. In Milgram's experiment, 65 per cent of instructors administered very high intensity electric shock. In Zimbardo's famous Stanford Prison Experiment, participants terminated their participation only after six days. These two classic experiments highlight that submission and obedience can easily transform some normal people into instruments of torture.

A key point in Plutchik's analysis is the nature of combination. Trust is essential for developing followership, but accompanying it with fear or with joy can result in very different kinds of followers. We all need to dissect emotions and see the best combinations that can be used to motivate ourselves and others.

Emotional Equations

Based on the construct of emotional combinations, the entrepreneur, speaker and author Chip Conley (2012) suggests a number of emotional equations. These are helpful for achieving our professional and life goals. Three of them are congruent with viewpoints of modern, brain-based leadership.

1. Curiosity = Wonder + Awe

Curiosity is a prerequisite for creativity. It allows brain to process new information and challenge old biases. While wonder is the pure excitement of discovery, awe is fear and surprise combined. In order for our leadership curiosity to work well, we need to allow the pleasure of being faced with something potentially amazing, a new product/service, colleague technology, to go hand in hand with humility. Awe allows us to connect with the world around us and adopt a more realistic view.

2. Regret = Disappointment + Responsibility

Within dynamic business environments, leaders are

expected to make many decisions daily. Although some of these decisions have higher weight than others, choices are usually plentiful for each decision and choosing one alternative over others can emotionally backfire. The equation suggests that the higher the disappointment, your responsibility, or both, the higher the regret. Regret itself, according to Conely, is not necessarily a damaging emotion but if it turns to remorse (extreme regret) then it can be devastating.

3. Thriving = Frequency of positive / frequency of negative

Thriving, or positivity is about the relation between positive and negative events in our lives. In order for this equation to have a positive outcome, positive events have to outnumber negative events by three to one. This is because negativity has a stronger pull on us than positivity. Changing our perspective to start noticing more positive information around us, making sure we operate under the right values, appreciate any lesson from any event, and connect ourselves to other positive people can help us increase the nominator and decrease the denominator in this equation.

Bliss Leadership

Claudia Hammond (2005), in her book *Emotional Rollercoaster*, mentions that happiness is usually at the top of the list of people's aspirations. Incidentally prior assumptions considered satisfaction to be a core measurement for employees and customers. This management idea found its limit in one of the most popular paradigms that emerged in the 80s, called total quality management (TQM). Satisfaction alone cannot lead to the heightened behaviours we want ourselves and our employees to demonstrate. It seems that satisfaction has become, most of the time, a necessary but not sufficient condition for increased engagement and boosted loyalty. Satisfaction has a new meaning today because of uncertainty. It is observed that satisfaction itself has become a hygiene factor rather than a motivator.

No great leader will be ever remembered because of creating a satisfying working environment. Satisfaction is not enough. Great leaders are great because they can spread strong and heart-quickening, positive emotions, more specifically happiness.

Moving towards a more positive view of the mind is necessary to start taking things seriously. Happiness (or joy, or subjective well-being, or psychological well-being) becomes the positive emotion of choice in both science and pop culture. For both the wider society and organizations, the study of happiness brings a surprising and powerful insight. Happiness is not just an outcome of successful work, but a prerequisite. The counter intuitive finding goes against existing values since in many cultures around the world one is entitled to happiness only after success is secured. However, Boehm and Lyubomirsky (2008) have found substantial evidence to support of the reverse hypothesis (happiness is the reason why some employees are more successful than others). They conclude: "Taken together, the evidence suggests that happiness is not only correlated with workplace success but that happiness often precedes measures of success and that induction of positive affect leads to improved workplace outcomes.

Simon Achor, the global advocate for happiness at work, summarizes relevant research in his best-selling *The Happiness Advantage* book (2010). On the basis of his study involving 1,600 high achieving undergraduates at Harvard, he claims that "it turns out that our brains are literally hardwired to perform at their best not when they are negative or even neutral, but when they are positive. Yet on today's world, we ironically sacrifice for success only to lower our brain's success rate. Our hard-driving lives leave us feeling stressed, and we feel swamped by the mounting pressure to succeed at any cost.

Generally, we allow the negative emotions to get hold of us and we postpone happiness. This is exactly the happiness-averse mindset that makes success more difficult and more remote. What we need to do is the opposite. Regardless of the current conditions, we need to retain our high spirit and always strive for the best. This, mathematically, can lead to success more easily than negative or neutral emotions that we mind find more fitting for difficult times. This is why effective leaders try to create the best possible uplifting conditions. Recent analyses of cases of organizations struggling to survive in high crisis environment show that managers and leaders focused on the positive outcomes and emotions achieved better results (Psychogios & Szamosi, 2015). Happiness sets the foundation of success in any project because of its ability to release intelligence, creativity, commitment and collaboration.

Professor and author Richard Wiseman (2009), after reviewing the available literature on improving happiness, suggest these three fastest and surest routes for boosting happiness.

1.   **Gratitude and appreciation.** Happiness starts from the inside out and thus it needs a sunny place to start with. Create this sunny place by periodically expressing gratitude for everything good that has happened to you. If possible, create a written account of them. Frequently refresh your memory of fantastic

experiences (savouring) and relive the sensation within your mind. Do not hold back appreciation for those close to you; thank them for their contributions and efforts.

2. **Experience and sharing.** Our brains are hardwired to react to real-life experiences better than to our material belongings. So, in order to boost your happiness, start engaging in refreshing and rewarding experiences, as soon as possible. Also, create and offer such experiences to your team, not just material rewards. The 2015 results of Fortune's Top 100 Best Companies to Work for (Colvin, 2015) suggested that the free perks and futuristic offices are not the decisive factors. The key factor is the ability to foster strong, rewarding, relationship …. among their employees. Non-financial acts of kindness can substantially increase our happiness.

3. **Body language and behaviour.** A happiness inducing experiment can be performed. It includes holding a pen with your teeth. If you hold a pen horizontally in your teeth without touching it with your lips for few seconds your brain immediately releases happy hormones just because it thinks you are smiling. Since you are smiling, smoothing good must be happening. On the contrary, if you hold the end of the pen with your lips forming an O and not touching it with your teeth, your brain believes you are frowning and releases stress hormones. This shows that there is a two-way communication process between the brain and the body. It is not only what the brain feels, the body will show, but the other way around too. Smiling more, adopting a more confident, positive and upright body positive, using more positive wording when speaking and generally acting more happily will tell the brain to behave

accordingly. Be the change you want to see; be the happiness you want to feel.

Concluding Remarks

While positive emotions and happiness have been stressed in view of their significance in our lives and organizations, the adaptive value of negative emotions must have to be recognized. Todd Kashadan, a renowned expert on negative emotion and a few other positive psychologists advocate wholeness as the key to emotional success. They see both positive and negative as part of the larger, and more visible whole. For them, it is only wholeness that can lead to real emotional agility, which is not about avoiding negative emotions but about 'taking the negative out of them' (Biswas-Diener, 2015).

Applying Tomkins' Model in Organization
Dealing with positive emotions·

1. *Celebrate.* With any success, even the smallest, organize a celebration both for yourself and your team. The size and type of celebration should be related to the size and type of success. Share the joy and your team will share it inside and outside.

2. *Explore.* In accordance with the growth mindset, new data, people, situations should be looked at with excitement. Panksepp, the world's authority in affective neuroscience, has indicated that in the model of seven primary emotions (seeking, rage, fear, lust, care, panic/grief, play), seeking is probably the strongest one. It is the seeking circuit firing in the brain when we get excited from new intellectual connections, novel ideas, and cutting-edge technologies. **Dealing with neutral emotions**

---

3. *Stop-and-think.* When experiencing sudden, unexpected and sad event, it is proper to consider the situation closely before taking action. Stop and give time to yourself and your team.
   Dealing with negative emotions
4. *Recharge.* The brain reacts with anger when there are too many threats. When feeling rage, just ask yourself whether this is actually all about an overburdened brain.
5. *Alert.* When situation seems unfavourable, keep quiet during distress or try to ignore the problem. Reach out and alert your colleagues.
6. *Reassure.* Leaders may face failures. It takes willpower and a strong growth mindset to reassure yourself and your team.
7. *Double*-check. The experience of disgust may lead to contempt and alienating people. It is better to double-check where this response comes from. Is it because of burnout-induced cynicism, stereotype and other biases.

Chapter 11

Human Connectivity

E conomists and behavioural scientists in the past stressed the concept of 'selfish gene' and highlighted the role of competition. However, the new hyper socially wired lives we lead, and the unpredictability and dynamism of everyday work at the organization, require a different type of relationship. Creative solution to chaotic and complex new problems ask for closer, deeper and stronger types of relationships within and between groups. The 'I am a lone ranger, I trust no one, I succeed by myself' philosophy that probably worked well in some earlier decades cannot be applied anymore.

Is the best human strategy for success one of cooperation or conflict? Economists and behavioural scientists tried to answer this question through many theoretical constructs, most notably a gaming technique, **prisoner's dilemma**. Although conceived to prove that humans are better off non-collaborating than collaborating, in real life it actually proves the opposite. The mindset of a lone ranger or a lone wolf succeeding in all arenas and winning all challenges is an outdated and very dangerous one. While there are cases where our individual contribution is more desired and effective than a collective one, such cases are progressively becoming the exception and not the rule. *The good news is that our brain is profoundly wired for collaboration and social bonding,* and *that by* *understanding the neurological and behavioural underpinnings of cooperation we can reap benefits faster and better than ever before.* Our brains are inherently very good at it.

Prisoner Dilemma Game

The prisoner's dilemma is used by some economists as a mental exercise to show that selfish behaviour is preferable to cooperation. However, the renowned economist Amartya Sen (Noble Memorial Prize in Economics, 1998) has said, 'the purely economic man is indeed close to being a social moron'.

The prisoner dilemma (PD) game is simple. Two people have just been arrested by the police. They have been separated and offered two options in their interrogation rooms: they can either stay silent (the 'cooperate' strategy) or confess their crime (the 'defect' strategy). The consequences of these choices are the following:

- If both remain silent (so both choose to cooperate) they are only charged with a minor crime and exit first in a year
- If they both confess (so both choose to defect) they each get five years in jail.
- If one confesses and the other doesn't (one defects and one cooperates) then the confessor is free and the other gets 10 years.

Prisoner 1

	Confess	Does not confess
Confess **Prisoner 2**	5 year prison term for both	Prisoner 1 gets 10 years prisoner 2 goes free
Does not Confess	Prisoner 2 gets 10 years Prisoner 1 goes free	1 year term for both

The celebrated, Noble Laureate economist Joh Nash opines that the best possible and rational strategy is not to cooperate. However, this not what happens in reality. Thaler (2015), one of the fathers of behavioural economics, offers a different view. According to him, 40-50% of the players cooperate when the game is played in the laboratory. This means that cooperation is not discarded.

The main problem with the PD game is that players cannot communicate, they cannot change their mind, and they do not really know each other. In reality and especially in the business and managerial situations we face daily, all these conditions are actually in reverse. In many situations, we know people and they know us. Thus, the best strategy is to cooperate. Even in jail-related situations, cooperation seems to the default strategy. In a WIRED magazine article about two caught Las Vegas gamblers who managed to illegally hack the algorithm of electronic games in casinos, it was reported that when law officers offered them a version of the prisoner's dilemma in order to push them to confess, they actually remained silent and walked free a few months later (Caparo, 2013). The prisoner's dilemma for humans suggests collaboration.

Based on relevant findings and suggestions, here are specific strategic steps for modern managers to maximize the positive effects of cooperation.

- *Be nice: Never defect fact, always start by cooperating.* If you defect first, people will take it as your default strategy and they will approach you with extreme caution. In difficult negotiations, in meetings with people you don't know and in interaction with people outside the company always start by offering your partnership by demonstrating goodwill. In that way you increase the possibility of them cooperating as well.

- *Retaliate / reciprocate: If they defect, defect too.* Do not allow a hostile move to go unnoticed. By defecting when they do, you give a strong message 'I am not a fool; do not take me for granted'. If they cooperate, cooperate too without a second thought.
- *Be forgiving.* Defect when they do but after they show goodwill again, be forgiving. This is the only way to get out of a vicious circle of defections. Forgiving and demonstrating a will for better future relations is a winning strategic choice.
- *Communicate: Reality-based dilemma occurs everyday lives do not require people to be isolated in detention cell.* Actively exchange reliable information.
- *Be non-envious:* Focus on maximizing your own score and not necessarily on the best total score in one round.

The Socially Wired Brain

How important are social connections on our lives for who we are, how we behave and what we achieve? Is our brain a personal score-maximizing machine or a collective-balancing one? Should we only care about ourselves or should we spend our valuable brain energy on others too? Ultimately, is leadership an individual or a social game? Such questions are central to the **BAL (brain-adaptive leadership model)** since increasing evidence from neuroscience, psychology and sociology suggest that *'WE' is more important than 'I'*. A leader who cannot understand and connect meaningfully with the brains of others is a leader doomed to fail.

Our brain is a social organ. Social relationships have a dramatic impact on a large number of brain functions and connections, and ignoring them or downgrading them can only harm our overall leadership performance. The mere fact that we have a consciousness, observing and reflecting on our actions and on the surrounding world, is because of our social dimensions. Eminent psychologists and neuroscientists attribute the very existence of consciousness to social relationships. According to Halligan and Oakley (2015), "consciousness simply occurs too late to affect the outcomes of the mental processes apparently linked to it. We suggest it is the product of our unconscious mind, and proceeds an evolutionary advantage that developed for the benefit of the social group, not the individual".

This is an amazing statement. The very thing that seems to make us different from each other and even egoistic in our behaviour, the uniqueness of our conscious thinking, is actually a brain function developed by the unconscious to help us survive as a social group not as an individual. The 'WE' created the 'I'. How contradictory it sounds in the light of the profound individualism we observe in our organizations and personal lives. According to Halligan and Oakley (2015), our unconscious mind broadcasts all information and decisions to our conscious mind that then creates a personalized construction necessary for developing adaptive strategies in the real world – such as the predicting the behaviour of others, disseminating selected information and being able to adjust perceptions based on external stimuli.

Neuroscientist Michael Graziano also posits similar views. His *Attention Schema Theory* argues that we have our consciousness in order to detect the consciousness of other people. We perceive awareness in other people. This is crucial to us as social animal. We are wired to use our attention to unconsciously detect signs in the other people's verbal and body language in order to better understand their state of mind and act accordingly. This is who it is called the Attention Schema Theory: we use part of our attention span to pick up patterns on other people's thinking, feeling and doing.

Another Professor of Psychology and author of the book *The Neuroscience of Human Relationships*, Cozolino (2006) emphasized that the brain and the body are biological organisms. They are social organisms such as the neuron in the brain is a social organism. It needs to connect with other neurons'. If people, and neurons, fail to create adequate connections across the social domain or across the brain respectively, they can be isolated or even rejected from the social and neuro system respectively with probably negative outcomes. A neurons need to create new pathways for the brain to remain healthy and to thrive, people need to create new relationships in order to remain healthy and to thrive. In order for neuroplasticity to work and to create novel neural pathways our brain needs to be adequately stimulated. If this does not happen we have less chances for growth. Cozolino concludes, "We are beginning to realize that we're not separate beings, that we are all just members of a hive, and it may take centuries to realize that we're much more interconnected than what we realize now" (Sullivan, 2015).

The more a leader gets disconnected from its overall environment, the more leaders become ineffective. Our brain is primarily a connecting, interacting, trusting and cooperating organ and there is the evolution of human kind to provide the testimonial for it. Actually, our species' unique ability to form multi-layered social relations and to collaborate within highly complex and coordinated group activities with genetically unrelated individuals makes the single most important difference for us. Marean, Director of the Institute of Human Origin at the Arizona State University, believes firmly that Homo Sapiens' extraordinary ability to cooperate, what he calls hyperprosociality, is not a learned tendency but a genetically encoded trait. Although cooperation is also observed in primate species, our unique ability to cooperate is large.

Studies have shown that chimps and young human children perform equally on typical IQ tests but human offsprings do much better on tests related to social-cognitive skills, like learning from each other. So, when someone brags about the power of competition in fueling personal, economic and social growth, just remind them that without our brain's propensity for cooperation, mutual learning and social fairness would go extinct. *People tend to think of evolution as a strictly dog-eat-dog struggle for survival. In fact, cooperation has been a driving force in evolution.*

Leaders in organizations cannot go on with a mental state of fierce competition or a feeling of isolation from their social surrounding. On the contrary, wholeheartedly embracing collaboration and cooperation, alongside the necessary competitions and unavoidable conflicts, will advance them to true brain adaptive leaders.

The Capacity to Mentalize (Theory of Mind)
The ability of our brain to understand other people's mental states and to use this information to predict their behaviour is really astonishing. It is also an extremely helpful tool for managers and leaders in all organizations around the world. Neuroscience and psychology call this ability **Theory of Mind (ToM)** and it represents a core skill of our social brain. The foundations for this theory were laid down in the late 1970s when Premack and Woodruff (1978) asked in their seminal paper 'Does the chimpanzee have a theory

of mind?' They explained that an individual has a theory of mind if he imputes mental states to himself and others. A system of this kind is properly viewed as a theory because such states are not directly observable, and the system can be used to make prediction about the behaviour of others. The most famous test of ToM involves a scenario like this. Imagine two children, Sally and Anne, sitting side by side and holding one box each. Sally also holds a stone, which she places into her box and then she leaves the room without her box. While Sally is away, Anne opens Sally's box, takes the stone out, and places in her box. Upon Sally's return participating children are asked to predict in which box Sally will look back her for her stone. If the answer is in her own box, then the children correctly recognized Sally's individuality of mind. If they answer that Sally will look into Anne's box, then they fail the test.

ToM research showcases the importance of mind reading for human understanding, learning and collaborating – mind reading not in a supernatural way, but in a very human, brain-based ability to hypothesize what another person is thinking. *Shared intentionality* is necessary in developing a common ground between members of a group, helping them to achieve point attention and ultimately so act cooperatively towards a collective goal.

The ability to understand the state of mind of the people across the table and to decide their intentions is key to successful decision making. (It is important to recognize that autistic children and adults do not possess theory of mind). This is the true expression of healthy brain senergy within a team. The whole is greater than the sum and a few minds interacting together produce better outcomes than individuals and isolated thinking.

The Mirrors in Our Brain

In 1992, Italian researchers published a study showing that a macaque's neurons fired, not only when the monkey was performing an action but also when the monkey was observing another one doing so. Since then, numerous studies appeared supporting and expanding on the **mirror neurons theory.** Celebrated supporters of the wider role that mirror neurons play in our individual lives, group workings and even in our culture include neuroscientists vs Ramachandran (2011), who believes that the discovery of mirror neurons is equal in significance to the discovery of DNA, and Icoboni (2009) who claims that mirror neurons are the special brain cells that can finally help us answer century-old philosophical and scientific questions regarding cultures and societies.

In the leadership literature arena, Goleman and Boyatzis (2008) published HBR articles titled "Social intelligence and the biology of leadership". for them, mirror neurons play an important role in leadership effectiveness since following of the leader will copy or mirror the leader's mental state based on how the leader expresses it.

The whole concept of *empathy* is based on mirror neurons. Lead-by-example is now more relevant than ever due to the amazing role of mirror neurons. Mirror neurons can work miracles if we choose to acknowledge them and use them in the right directions daily in our working lives.

Human Connectivity

Leaders are not, or should not be islands. They should be actively connected to people inside and outside their organizations, with those close to them but also with those further away from their immediate personal circle. We see the creation, maintenance and constant development of powerful human networks as an indispensable aspect of modern leadership in all organizations. This is because our brain, as a primarily information – processing organ needs the right sources and input of information in order for it to create great output in the form of ideas, emotions and actions.

The *classic social networks, theory* of 'the strength of weak ties' developed by American sociologist Granovetter in the beginning of the 1970s and advanced strongly since then, is an excellent mental tool for understanding and making better use of our personal connections in other people. Granovetter suggested that we need to urgently look at the ties between people that are *not* strong, in the sense of relationship proximity (that is, close family members, friends, and colleagues). In other words, we need to turn our attention to weak ties (acquaintances, distant friends, etc.). The argument goes that although strong ties are invaluable, weak ties inject necessary new ideas, new experiences and new practices in a group of people. Fresh ideas, strategic information, out-of-the-box innovations, change initiative and alternative perspectives come from weak ties.

In order for weak ties to work best they need to be qualitatively different from a simple 'friend-of-a-friend' connection. Based on Granovetter's ground-breaking work, a leadership network connection matrix has been proposed.

The Leadership Network Connection Matrix		
Type of Connection	Power of Connection	
	Dynamic/Productive	Static/Non productive
Strong/close	Active operational support	Potential dead-end
Weak/distant	Active strategic bridge	Potential beneficial link

Weak ties that are active and productive, supply crucial strategic information to the leader and to the team, and thus are instrumental in introducing change and innovation. Leaders should be proactive in creating such connections since this is a core responsibility of the leadership role. For example, they need to attend events such as conferences, seminars and fairs with an open mind and a proactive approach to be able to create new contacts. That's the first step. The second step is to invest personal time to nurture those contacts in order to keep them active. Weak ties that exist but are not utilized are potential bridges and although not much time is to be spend on them, they should remain within the leader's mental radar and reach. Strong ties are to be maintained for everyday support network.

The Art of Human Connectivity

Brafman and Brafman (2010) suggest a five-step continuum for everyday conversation and connectivity.

1. **Phatic stage:** We speak with social niceties, words void of emotional change such as 'how are you?' and 'nice to see you'.

2. **Factual stage:** We speak with actual facts and data that do not elicit any subjective option, such as 'I am an Engineer' or 'I live in Bhubaneswar'.

3. **Evaluative stage:** We speak with personal views and opinions, such as 'I like this scheme' and 'the product is amazing'.

4. **Gut-level stage:** We speak in emotionally revealing statements like 'I am so happy that Ravi has joined our company'.

5. **Peak stage:** This is the most revealing stage where we open our heart and mind, and speak about our inner feelings, deep concerns and widest hopes.

Statements such as 'I really wonder how we are going to make this month with so low numbers ……..

Leaders are not islands. On the contrary, they take central positions in organization and business networks in order to facilitate relations that will help them achieve their goals. However, they need to recalibrate their brains to better understand the social behaviours of themselves and others, and to constantly connect deeper with people both inside and outside their organizations. Fully appreciating the socially based origins of consciousness, and adopting a 'collaborative first and then reciprocate' attitude are necessary conditions towards adapting our brains for effective leadership.

Chapter 12

Stress and Resilience

"Worry affects the circulation, the heart, the glands, the whole nervous system. I have never known a man who died from overwork, but many who died from doubt."

- Charles Horace Mayo

In March 2011, Antonio Hotta-Osorio, a young star in the finance world became the youngest of Britain's Big Five bank CEO, heading Lloyds Banking Group. His arrival on the scene led to tremendous hope for Lloyds – which was facing substantial number of problems. Antonio worked tirelessly, often logging marathon ninety-four weeks to turn the bank around.

Eight months after Antonio took on the high-power, high-pressure CEO position at Lloyds, he took a medical leave of absence due to extreme stress and fatigue. His stress was so high that he was unable to sleep for five days running. When the news of his leave of absence hit, Lloyds lost one billion sterling in market value. As in Antonio's case, stress can backfire and prevent us from achieving our goals.

Stress
Stress is experienced when demands exceed the resources (happens when people feel under threat):
- Frightened by change, uncertainty
- Self-esteem is attacked

- Demands (both internal and external) are beyond control or capability to meet

We are currently in an era where the pace of change and financial uncertainty has created an unprecedented rise in stress. We are beginning to understand the breadth and depth of the **consequences.** Stress affect our:

- **Thoughts:** Difficulty in concentration on creativity; worrying about position, depressed self-esteem
- **Emotions:** Anger and irritability; difficulty in releasing pent-up emotions
- **Behaviour:** Appear short-tempered and grumpy; locked away in office and unavailable for visitors.
- **Physical symptoms:** Clenched jaw, grinding teeth, headache, back pain, too much sleep or too little sleep

The astounding cost of work related stress to economy has reached a massive level. An astounding number of work days are lost; employees come to work disengaged, tired, unmotivated and too stressed. The rise of chronic diseases, obesity and stress in the modern world are well known but there is also evidence of a rise in the incidence of more acute events due to stress, such as heart attacks. There is now clear knowledge that stress, even in the absence of chronic risk factors such as high blood pressures, cholesterol or smoking, leads to more heart disease and strokes.

There are several mechanisms by which how you feel affects your health – chemical or hormonal (arising from the endocrine system), nervous (arising from the brain, spinal cord or peripheral nervous system) or psychological (coming from your thoughts and perceptions).

Stress triggers the production of some of the most powerful chemicals that affect how your brain and body work.

Adrenalin from our adrenal glands (sitting just above

your kidneys) is often correlated with increased "sympathetic" activity in the autonomic nervous system commonly recognized as the "fight, fright, flight" or short-term stress response.

Cortisol (from another part of our adrenal glands but stimulated by the hypothalamic-pituitary axis in the brain) is associated with longer term or chronic stress responses.

Cortisol

The steroid hormone cortisol is a key part of our stress hormone. It mobilizes our energy, affect the immune system and essentially enables the brain to cope better with the stimuli that have created the stress. We know that a level of challenge can be beneficial, heightening our ability to respond to stressors. Chronic, sustained, unavoidable stress, which stimulates an excess of cortisol is very harmful, and can lead to cell death in the brain, and even, in extreme situations, to death. Indeed, chronic stress has symptoms very similar to aging in the brain, and excessive cortisol causes significant damage to the hippocampus, crucial to the retention of memory.

Although there is some evidence that mild stress (good stress) plays a role in adaptive changes in the immune system, chronic and long lasting stress causes damaging changes in the immune system.

These chemicals affect the brain directly, but they can also affect immune system, and the vague nerve, which connects the digestive system and the brain. Experience of stress, sustained over long periods of time can have a powerful and widespread negative impact on our thinking, feeling, health and hence productivity.

Highly intelligent and stressful people easily grasp that

what we eat, do or do not drink, how well we sleep and whether we exercise affect our health.

Dealing with Stress

Remedies are sought after the event. However, a more fundamental question concerns: what can we do as leaders to avoid the build-up of stress?

First of all, having understood stress and its effects, we can avoid being the cause of it ourselves, and create cultures, structures, and environments that make it easier for others to deal with stress. Stress is envitable in highly competitive and developed global economies. So we should develop our own and others' resilience through "role-modeling" healthy behaviours. A number of helpful strategies are indicated below:

- Physical exercise to release adrenalin and cortisol from our sweat and redress the balance with the endorphins such as serotonin released by aerobic activity
- Journaling to release the negative effects of survival emotions from our mind
- Discussion with a close confidante, mentor, friend or coach.
- Ensure getting good quality sleep
- Manage commute to make it a time that you can recharge rather than an extra stress in your day
- Do not succumb to fueling stress with caffeine, alcohol or high sugar products
- Supplement your diet with magnesium and omega oils that keep your brain healthy
- Any form of meditation (especially yoga nidra)

Secondly, we should be aware of our mindset, behaviour and feelings. It is observed that most senior positions have less stress than those with less autonomy, perhaps because they are better at managing their responses. Leaders need to recognize that unrealistic optimism can be just as damaging as pessimism. A crucial part of leadership role is to develop stories and strategies that reframe the future so as to reduce uncertainty for others.

Thirdly, be sensitive to the signs of stress in others. As a leader you need to be adapt at tuning into others' emotions as well as in managing your own. In times of great change and turbulence, knowing when to suggest a supportive intervention such as coaching might make all the difference to a key person.

Finally, choose any intervention carefully. There is evidence that cognitive behaviour stress management (CBSM) can reduce stress response. It makes sense that psychology is the top choice to see leaders and their organizations through tough times. The mind does not reside only in the brain; it resides in the body too. The mind-brain-body relationship is fluid and mutually inclusive.

CBSM is a short-term therapeutic approach that focuses on how people's thoughts affect their emotions and behaviours. It attempts to influence a client's irrational thoughts while focusing directly on identifying and changing behaviours and thought patterns. CBSM provides opportunity for psychologists to provide information, build a client's emotional and interpersonal skills, and support them through the process. During CBSM a client learns recovery skills that are useful throughout their lifetime. Techniques and skills that are acquired during CBSM help facilitate sustained behaviour change and have been shown to decrease the sense of isolation and depressive symptoms while improving immunity.

Resilience

Why does resilience matter? You may recollect your own experiences. You maintained your stellar track record when the market was on rise, customers had plenty of cash and desire for your product, the team was fresh and full of enthusiasm, and there was plenty of room for growth and development. You are now challenged by a situation dominated by:

- The lag in confidence after a global recession
- A mature market with emerging innovations
- A mature team competing

Alternatively, you have just stalled due to:

- A personal setback
- Illness or injury
- A death or sickness in the family
- Threats to your status

It has been shown that people in higher positions of authority have lower levels of cortisol and lower anxiety. Leadership is thus associated with lower levels of stress. In view of this observation, it is proposed that a key factor in the lower stress levels the greater sense of control, a psychological resource known to have a stress buffering effect.

So the ability to manage stress, in particular, to have the resources to avoid or modulate long lasting stress, seems a most beneficial trait for leadership. *Resilience refers to the capacity of preventing or minimizing the adverse impact of negative environment.*

Building Resilience

Although there is evidence that the baseline to which we manage stress is largely set in early childhood, it is increasingly accepted that we can develop resilience, improving our responses to stress and thus our ability to manage it.

A number of personal characteristics are conducive to managing responses to stress.

- Openness to new tasks and new people
- A greater tendency towards attachment emotions
- Feeling in control
- Not having high levels of anxiety
- Being secure in one's status
- Realistic optimism
- The ability to adapt by reframing stressful events and situations
- Close, supportive personal relationships

Other environmental factors also seem to help such as:

- A stable, safe society
- Good quality schools
- Sufficient resources

Being able to regulate emotion is a useful tool for leaders. In addition to *reframing* (actively seeking to find more positive ways of interpreting stressful events and situations), a few other techniques listed below are very useful.

- **Mindfulness meditation** – focusing on the present or a single focus (commonly breath) which brings about an incredible and pervasive sense of well-being with regular practice
- **Compassionate meditation** – opening up the heart and mind towards good will, appreciation and equanimity to others (and yourself)
- **Transcendental meditation** – Using a sound or mantra which you repeat 15-20 minutes per day as a

method of relaxation, stress reduction, and self-development.

- **Cognitive bias modification** (CBSM) training can help develop a more realistically outlook

Another recommendation is to gradually increase the stress challenge we face so that our sense of efficacy and confidence grow as we learn to deal with stress in a controlled way. Sometimes called **stress inoculation,** this technique is widely used in training in the military and other front line services.

It used to be said that to be a good leader of a large organization, you needed to have managed a team before the age of 30, giving a lot of time for practice, for learning from mistakes and building confidence as teams get larger and management demands more complex. What we now know about neuroplasticity means you can teach an "older" dog new tricks so fear not if you are closer to 50 or 60 or even 70. Again successful change depends on sustained practice, worth remembering as yet another good lesson for delegation, especially when you are trying to develop resilience in others.

Building stronger supportive and trusting relationships also helps, as we know that warm relationships help release oxytocin, which suppresses the release of cortisol. One way of looking at your relationships is through the creation of a network map, with the thickness of the lines representing the strength of the relationship.

- Have you got the right kind of support around you?
- Do you have a mentor outside the organization you can turn to?
- Are you a key node in your subordinates' network, helping them become resilient?

- Do you have a handful of good, close friends, family or confidants you can discuss your worst-case scenarios with?

Another known way of improving one's emotional states or moods is to be altruistic, to think of others and be active in contributing to a community or to count one's blessings, regularly, perhaps once a day, remember the good things and people in your life that you are grateful for.

Finally, remember the extent to which your body and mind are part of the same system, indeed one system. Standing tall, playing the role, walking the walk of a confidant leader is known to boost testosterone levels and reduce cortisol. Your body language shapes who you are. It emphasizes that two minutes of standing in the power pose boasts confidence (and testosterone).

Actions and Reflections

- **Turn to list** – make a list of people in your life that you can turn to for help, comfort or reassurance should you need it. Knowing that they have a safe harbour for times of need makes people feel more securely attached to the world.
- **Gratitude list** – list ten things you are grateful for. Trying to do this every day or most days of the week. This would help you to draw on the necessary resources without feeling totally drained.

Chapter 13

Difference, Diversity and Gender

A growing body of research links economic performance to diversity. "Diversity bonus" is found for diverse management. A diverse management is linked to more product innovation, a diverse workforce is better at reaching diverse markets and there are positive links between a migrant population and entrepreneurship. One of the most powerful benefits of a diverse workforce and inclusive and diverse leadership appears to be increased innovation and better flow from ideas to market. A number of reasons have been put forward as to why diversity should be so useful.

Plasticity and Epigenetics (The Engines of Differences)
    The evidence for brain plasticity adds to our emerging knowledge of *epigenetics,* the science of environmental changes to the behaviour or expression of genes. We must change the language around nature versus nurture, genetic code versus environment. We have already gathered the information that some of the ways in which our environment, primarily relationships with other people, as well as our own decisions and actions, shape our brain. Our genetic code is not just an immutable blueprint, or hardwired system, but a working plan adaptable, or vulnerable, to changing internal and external circumstances.

In the womb, the different experiences and environments are already beginning to shape our brains, our bodies and we are as people, into entirely unique entities. Identical twins with an identical genetic code are still born with difference and acquire even more of them throughout life.

During the second World War, in the winter of 1944-45, the west of Holland experienced a period of extreme food shortage (the Hunger Winter). Researchers have looked into its effects. It showed how the near starvation conditions of pregnant mothers caused changes in how genes in their babies would be expressed later in life, with observable differences up to 60 years later. For example, when babies were born to mothers who were starved in the first three months of pregnancy but had access to better food in the later months, they were born with normal weights but had a tendency of obesity in later life, and their children in turn were more likely to be heavier than average at birth.

So our genomes, our physical, social and cultural environments, as well as thoughts, actions, habitual behaviours and heritable genetic changes, contribute to shaping who we are: our bodies, identities, our non-conscious and conscious assumptions, our perceptions, our attitudes, the frame to our world view, the breadth and depth of our knowledge and expertise, what others see as our character and nature, what we experience as our self. Such is the ability of the brain to change itself or be sculpted by every encounter.

The Diversity Bonus

Diverse people bring not only diverse views but different sets of knowledge. Diversity comes from life experiences as well as culture, race and gender. A challenging personality can also bring valuable skepticism or provoke new thinking. The surprise/ startle effect of hearing from someone with an entirely different world view can motivate a broader search for relevant information and stimulate creativity.

A 300-year-old charitable organization was facing a future when its charitable purpose was no longer visible. The board recognized it needed to change, but with members who shared a lot of experience, no fixed term of office and whose average age was over 65, no change had been agreed over a two-year period. A new director, coming from another sector, recruited a number of new trustees – some much younger, some from different fields – and enabled the board to have much more robust discussions and agree a new, bold, strategy within months.

Being faced with the unexpected and unpredictable might cause the brain to experience a certain amount of discomfort – sometimes called *dissonance.* However, dissonance or discomfort might provoke curiosity, might be cause for focusing attention and hence energy on understanding the cause and avoiding it in future. This may encourage more openness and greater propensity to try new ideas.

It has been found that creativity and innovation flourish in the climate of cross fertilization. Hence research organizations are now encouraging cross-disciplinary works. People with different expertise, experiences, skills, from different cultures, backgrounds and types of education working together towards common goals, but with sufficient freedom to find their own way to those goals, might have a better chance to improve the quality of organizational decision making and be more likely to be creative.

Even adversity may promote creativity. Challenge, adversity and even trauma appear to provoke creativity in some people, especially those with the 'openness to experience' personality trait and a high need for individuality. One explanation offered is that kind of experience shakes up previous beliefs and opens thinking to new ways. Kaufman (2014) contends that surprise startle emotion is a potentiator for enabling brain change.

Gender Difference

Looking rather like a walnut, the brain is divided into two halves by a midline, central fissure extending from the back to the front side of the brain. What the two halves for, and why evolution has created such a division, has intrigued neuroscientists for at least the past 200 years. Now some tentative answers are beginning to appear. These are far from clear cut. Michael Trimble simplifies matters by saying that the left side of the brain is for doing things that are pointing and propositional; the right side is concerned with urging and yearning. Another way of saying what would be that the left brain stores and uses what is known; the right brain is all the time on the look-out for what is new and engaging. From the right brain, once something that was new becomes familiar through use, it gets passed across into the left brain as something that is known, even "routinized" and which requires less conscious effort to use.

The two halves-hemispheres – are connected by a bridge of nerves fibers that together are called the *corpus collosum*. Women's brains are rather better endowed than men's in this area of the brain, with up to four times as many fibers in the corpus collosum. In shifting information between the two halves the female corpus collosum has been likened to a well maintained motorway with excellent traffic flow, while the male system can sometimes be like an overgrown weedy country lane. Things move with much more difficulty and much more slowly.

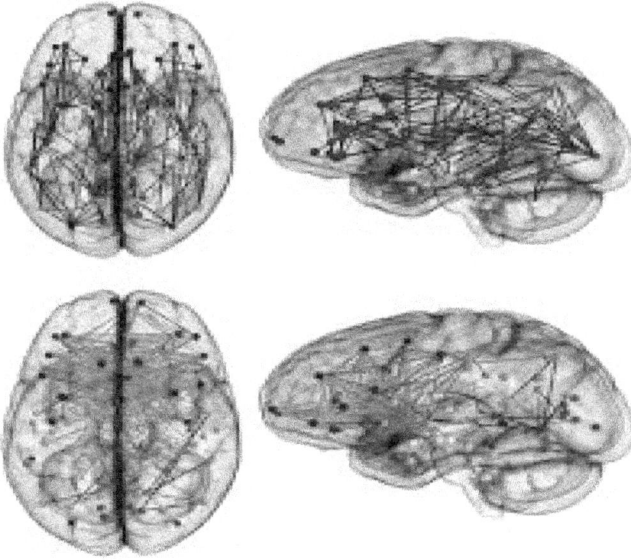

Figure: Male and female brain

The right brain deals with emotional information much more than the left brain, which likes facts. Sometimes the left brain is referred to as "the male brain" and the right brain as "the female brain". But it is over-simplification. However, men's brains are about 10 per cent bigger and contain 4 per cent more cells, but women's brains contain more neurons and more cellular connections. In terms of performance, the largest difference is in visual-spatial ability; there is male advantage in this skill.

The other major structural differences is the size of the limbic system – this is larger in the female brain, increasing women's ability to connect and bond with others. Some scientists using MRI have found that the prefrontal cortex is also larger. Most recently, in 2013, scientists from the University of Pennsylvania reported significant differences in the way men and women's brains tend to build their connections, using different tensor imaging (DTI). Whereas women's brains had more connections between hemispheres, men's brains had more connections within hemispheres. Men however had more connection between the right and left halves of the cerebellum. This fits with the earlier findings about women's larger corpus collosum and show possible explanations for men's superior coordination in movement and women's superiority in articulating their own emotions and understanding others'.

The Holistic Functions of Two Halves

A great synthesizing of modern knowledge about the two halves of the brain has been accomplished by neuroscientist, McGilchrist. According to him, brain is the place where "mind meets matter". The two halves of the brain deal with information differently. The left half deals with pieces of information in isolation, the right half with something as a whole. So right brain understands metaphor.

McGilchrist is clear that the most fundamental difference between the hemispheres is the type of attention they give to the world. That is important because if we are defined by what we see through what we attend to, then how we attend to and see things will have a huge effect upon who are and what we do.

The brain is not just a decision-making organ, not just the organ of relationship, not just a specialized kind of hardware or wetware. It is what makes the world. The world has no meaning except the meaning we assign to it. To do that well, both halves of the brain have to be integrated effectively; and that as not an easy task.

Structure is not the only way in which men and women's brain differ, although it is the best studied. There are chemical differences too; some major neurotransmitter receptors are distributed differently. Finally, there are functional differences. For example, the amygdala responds differently to acute and chronic stress in men and women, and also process emotional memories in different ways. Despite gender differences, men and women are still more similar as to their brains.

The brain works by innerconnection across several axes. The vertical axes (cortex, limbic, brainstem) deal with information moving from logical to emotional to physical; this can differ based on gender diversity. Generally speaking, women tend to have a richer vocabulary for emotions and men tend to push emotions into their bodies such that things like muscular tension, redness of the skin or raising of the voice are better indicators of mood. Women may cry more easily or their voice may become higher pitched but they are also more likely to be understanding and articulating what is destabilizing them. So to a large extent, understanding others means understanding how emotions are processed and expressed differently.

Information regarding gender difference has been derived from neuroscience and psychology. Yet we must be mindful of guarding against stereotypes. Traits like empathy vary with situations; gender difference may disappear. Some of the differences are innate: one-day-oldl female babies focus more on faces than males; even baby boy monkeys prefer cars and trucks to dolls. Both brain imaging and psychological research are leading to greater understanding of the differences between the sexes, but certainly in terms of functions, the overlap between men's and women's brains is greater than any difference.

Women and Leadership

Every thought is accompanied by some changes in the body through autonomic nervous system, partially related to adrenalin release, breathing, blood pressure, sweating and clenching fists. These often work through feedback loops so that changes in body can also change thoughts and decisions. Testosterone is a classic example. Men have more if it than women. Younger men have more of it than older men (it seems to drop over the age of 30). Men are more motivated by competition. While the significance of this observation has been used in sports, warfare and other competitive situations, women's sensitivity to context in relation to competition and risk calls for more women in top banking positions.

The issue of women leadership has become acute. Women still feel blocked, and a critical mass has not yet been achieved. In some of the empirical studies, women themselves perceived to the barriers for their career progression. Assertiveness, lack of sponsor, invisibility, lack of clarity and cultural barriers were reported as major hindrances.

Neuroscience has given us an understanding of the difference between individuals of all kinds due to the plasticity of their brains and the effect of environment on them, and of the value of diversity of thinking brings to organizations. This points to the need for women to stay true to their own values and styles of leadership, to be authentic. Trying to behave like a male leader will not help bring diverse views and experience. Trying to behave like a male leader will only work if that is a genuine expression of who you are – and there are many women who are indeed quite "masculine" in the way their brain works, just as there are men who are highly tuned into their right hemisphere and are seen as having a strong "feminine side". Otherwise it will cause internal conflict, which will be felt by others and undermine trust and impact.

Neuroscience is also showing some directions towards new models of leadership self-awareness and self-control, balance between intuition and consciously rational, logical thinking, the ability to communicate profoundly and understand the role of emotions, to manage stress, are all critical to effective leadership. human beings can learn these skills.

Actions and Reflections

- When conducting skills audit include measures for diversity and differences.
- Test your internal promotion and external recruitment process for transparency and ambiguity. How widely do you identify talent and potential?
- Ensure that you elicit, welcome and show gratitude for diverge views that challenge your thinking, especially when you disagree with them.
- Share your understanding of the benefits of diversity.

Chapter 14

Brain Agility and Engagement

The improvement and maintenance of brain fitness is a formidable challenge. Businesses are more focused than ever on excellent performance and acquiring a competitive edge through interventions such as executive coaching and leadership development. What can we learn from the London 2012 Olympics and Paralympics? As South African athlete Oscar Pistorius famously said, "every race is won or lost in the head". Pistorius, a double amputee, ran in both the Paralympics and Olympics but fell from grace when he was put on trial after a tragic shooting of his girlfriend, for which he was found guilty of culpable homicide. It was interesting to witness how our brains moved along the basic emotions spectrum during his trial in 2014, the shocking nature of the incidence moving us from the joy and excitement of the Olympics to anger, disgust and sadness.

In the business world we are increasingly aware of the importance of integrating logic and emotion via the left and right hemispheres of the brain. This may be an oversimplification, but the brain-body connection must not be underestimated.

Honing Our Senses

The five senses are how our brains know what is going on in our world.

- Smell – through olfactory nerve

- Taste – through facial and glossopharyngeal nerves
- Touch – Via somato sensory system
- Vision – via optic and oculomotor nerve
- Hearing – from our vestibulocochlear nerve

Smell

This is the most emotive sense because the olfactory nerve travels directly from the nose to a part of the brain that is close to some of the emotional centres, the limbic system. All the other senses involve nerves that travel around the skull before carrying information back to the brain. The hippocampus is the part of the brain where emotions are linked to memories and some peoples' most vivid memories are strongly associated with smell. The smell of the sea freshly cut grass and the damp smell of earth after it rains can invoke strong childhood memories.

Lavender is the most potent naturally occurring neuromodulator. It can balance the emotions calming people when they are agitated and invigorating when they are melancholic.

Taste

In terms of brain optimization, a cup of tea or coffee or a piece of chocolate bring ourselves back to the present. This is a form of mindfulness. When we are not mindful, challenge can deplete our resilient more markedly.

Touch

In terms of brain-body connection touch is about considering the information your largest organ-the skin – is providing you with. There is a map of the body in the sensory cortex of the brain called the *homunculus*. It appears somewhat distorted as the parts of the body with the most sensory neurons are most highly represented. So the lips and fingertips appear much larger than the arms and legs.

Finnish scientists have produced "Bodily maps of emotions" which shows where different emotions are manifested in the body across global cultures. The results have been reported in the *Proceeding of the National Academy of Sciences*.

Vision

This is probably the sense we use the most. Novelty is good for the brain so look out for something new every day. The *social neuroscience* tells us that the most eye contact occurs between two women, least between two men and moderate between a man and a woman. Eye contact is also one of the ways we build healthy neural architecture in our children. Romanian orphans who were fed, washed and clothed adequately but not given any cuddles or face-to-face contacts developed disorders and mental health problems.

One needs to look at eyes while shaking hand. Bill Clinton was particularly good at this.

Hearing

If you have a list of goals you are trying to achieve or behavioural habits you hope to embed, then try reading them out loud. When you read things out loud you use three parts of the brain, so it reinforces the message to your brain much more strongly than reading alone.

- Wernicke's area which understands written and spoken language
- Broca's area linked to speech production
- Temporal lobe which holds auditory centres
  We use this when coaching to save us repeating the

same message three times. It is also the reason that parents and teachers ask children to repeat things back to them. A rhythmical speaking style has positive effect. That's why we remember nursing rhymes or catchy slogans so well.

Brain Olympics

Attempts to maintain and promote brain agility require competitive strivings. In such competitive strivings, the following metaphors are appropriate:

- Bronze – Resilience
- Silver – Energy
- Gold – Higher purpose

Bronze Level

At the bronze level we need to ensure enough good quality sleep. Six to eight hours is recommended although this will vary from person to person. As long as we are waking up refreshed and dreaming enough, we are probably allowing sufficient time for the brain to rest and build up resources for resilience.

We should avoid these things as much as we can:

- Much of caffeine. Some people are especially sensitive to the effects of caffeine, others find no effect from it whatsoever and some people can drink a mug of it just before they go to bed. Try to work out which category you fall into.
- Use of substances such as nicotine and alcohol. These should be avoided generally and avoided altogether for two hours prior, to bed time as they stimulate the brain.
- Use of digital media should be ceased one hour before going to bed due to effects of unnatural light from the screen on the pineal gland and also the cognitive

stimulation from dealing with the information on the screens and you certainly should not be sleeping with your smart phone or device next to you due to the effects of wifi and 3G or 4G signals on your brain waves.

One of the most incredible findings from brain science research in 2012 was about how the brain cleans itself of toxic waste byproducts while we sleep. The "glymphatic" system relies on cerebrospinal fluid to flush out neurotoxins overnight, including one called beta amyloid which is found in clumps in the brains of people with Alzheimer's disease. This was followed up in 2013 by research that identified "hidden caves" that open in the brain while we sleep, allowing cerebrospinal fluid to flush out neurotoxins through the spinal column. The implications of this research cannot be overstated: failing to get enough sleep may prevent the brain from being able to remove neurotoxins that eventually lead to neurological disorders like Alzheimer's and Parkison's.

When brain is rested and resilient, one can:
- Perform better under pressure
- Regulate emotion
- Multitask
- Think flexibly and creatively
- Solve complex problems
- Be responsive to behavioural demands
- Make best decisions / choices

Silver Level

This is about doing all the above, as well as meeting healthy nutrition, hydration and basic exercise requirement.

Oxygenating your brain with exercise or at least deep breathing is essential. Recommendations would include doing 30 minutes of cardiovascular exercise on most days of the week. The serotonin boosting effect of this can be equivalent to the effect of a low dose of an anti-depressant and has been reported to boost productivity at work on the exercise takes place in the morning by as much as 15 per cent. Combined with the beneficial effects of fresh air and being exposed to sunlight, this has serious brain boosting power, as oxygen and glucose are vital fuels for the brain. The pineal gland needs sunlight to regulate our sleep-wake cycle and there are cascade effects on moods and stress level.

Glucose from a healthy, balanced diet rich in antioxidants and supplemented with vitamins and omega oils is important. The brain, although 2 per cent of body weight, consumes 20 per cent of its glucose intake in a critical "just in time" delivery system and cannot store glucose for later use. This should encourage the practice of regular eating to avoid defaulting. The brain is constantly scanning for threats and if there is not enough fuel available it will not be used to generate trust. You understand yourself or have lower levels of self-belief when not well-fed and watered.

Hydration is critical. A 1 to 3 per cent decrease in your hydration levels negatively affects your memory concentration and decision-making power. You need to drink at least 500 ml of water for every 15kg of your body weight, per day, and more if you are drinking lots of caffeine or sweating profusely.

Gold Level

With resilience and energy in place, work on to integration of the various brain areas involved in personal and professional development, there is time to move towards fine-tuning intuition, not only focusing attention but shifting that focus flexibly when required, unleashing innovative capacity and thinking about leaving a legacy. To achieve this, like any Olympian; the talented and ambitious leader's efforts would be boosted. You need to concentrate on brain-based techniques for sustainable behaviour change including mindfulness. Alvin Toffler says *"the illiterate of the 21st century will not be those who can't read or write, but those who cannot learn, unlearn and re-learn"*.

If you would like to be less forgetful, sleep better, not get as stressed and make better decisions, you could supplement your healthy balanced diet with antioxidants, B complex vitamins, vitamin D, magnesium, and omega oils that keep your brain and nervous system healthy. There is also evidence that green tea extract induces neurogenesis—growth of new neurons – in mouse brains. Although green tea does contain caffeine, it also contains high levels of catechins which are antioxidants with anti-inflammatory properties thought to be protective against diseases like Alzheimer's. Green teas also contain 1-theanine, which can induce alpha waves in the brain associated with better mood, cognition and lower stress.

The Leadership Brain Agility tool is based on utilizing thinking from six different parts or systems of your brain to improve the flexibility of your decision making, risk taking and leadership. It is important to hone your strength while remaining very aware of your development areas and realizing that your key stakeholders, clients, direct reports or family members may have various differing approaches to yourself. It is diversity of thought after all, that leads to step changes.

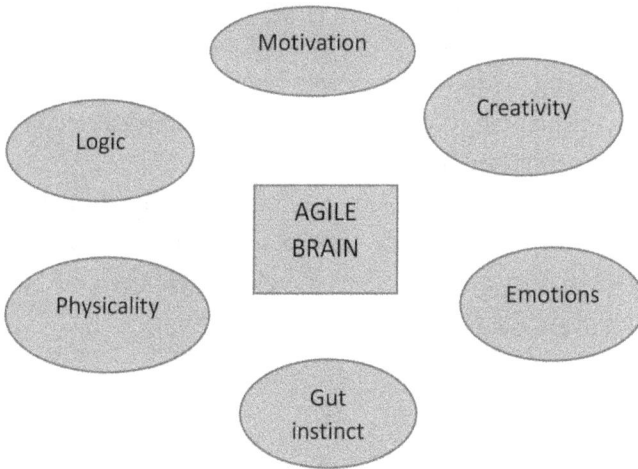

Motivation · Creativity · Logic · AGILE BRAIN · Physicality · Emotions · Gut instinct

Brain Agility Model

While it remains a gross over-simplification that the left correlates to logical, rational analytical thinking and the right to more creative, intuitive thinking, it is probably true that most people think predominantly in one of these ways, then has to more purposefully refer to the other way of thinking. Most right-handed people (80-90 per cent) have a dominant left-hemisphere, and left-handed people are about 50/50.

What mode of thinking do you think is primary for you, regardless of handedness.

Spiral Learning

Brain will struggle to take on more than two new habits at any one time, so the following spiral learning may be adopted:

- Pick one brain area and two habits relating to it or two brain areas to work on in the first instance.
- Once you have practiced that skill and it feels more

natural because it has become a habit, move on to one or two new brain areas or skills.

- Continue around the model in this way until you are comfortable that you could respond appropriately to different situations and people.
- Investing time in your agile brain is an essential key to sustainable leadership. Leaders who can surf ambiguity and learn adaptively will do better in future in the face of inevitably accelerating change.

Chapter 15

Neuroplasticity

Dogmas are not limited to day-to-day social life, there are also dogmas in the world of science. There is decades-old neuroscience dogma that the adult brain is essentially fixed in form and function. This dogma is wrong. Although distinct emotional styles reflect specific patterns of brain activity, emotional style is not a direct product of the genes people inherit from their parents but is instead a complex result of those genes plus the experience we had as children.

Instead the brain has the property called neuroplasticity, the ability to change the structure and patterns of activity in significant ways not only in childhood, which is not very surprising but also in adulthood and throughout life. The change can come about as a result of experiences we have as well as of purely internal mental activity – our thoughts.

Experience may take various forms. The brains of people who have been blind from birth and who learn to read by Braille, the writing system based on tiny raised dots that the fingers slide across, experience a measurable increase in the size and activity of areas in the motor cortex and somatosensory cortex that control movement and receive tactile sensation from the reading fingers. Even more dramatically, their visual cortex – which is normally hardwired to process signals from the eyes and turn them into visual images – undertakes a career change and takes on the job of processing sensation from the fingers rather than the inputs from the eyes.

Reading Braille is an example of intense, repeated sensory and learning experience of the outside world. But the brain can change in response to messages generated internally (our thoughts and intentions). These changes can increase or decrease the cortical real estate devoted to specific functions. Similarly, thoughts alone can increase or decrease activity in specific brain circuits that underlie psychological illness, as when cognitive-behaviour therapy successfully quiets the overactivity in the "worry circuit" which causes obsessive – compulsion disorder (OCD). By mental activity alone, itself a product of the brain, we can intentionally change our brain.

Hardwired Dogmas

The idea that there is a one-to-one correspondence between structure and function dates back 1861, when French anatomist Paul Broca announced that he had identified the brain region that produces speech. It is an area toward the back of the frontal Lobes, he concluded from the autopsy of a man who had lost essentially all the powers of speech. The brain's speech producing area is called Broca's area.

With that discovery, other brain scientists joined the race of identifying particular brain area for particular function. A German neurologist, Korbinian Brodmann, yielded structure-function relationships for fifty-two distinct regions. For example, Brodman area number 1 represents the parts of somatosensory cortex that processes tactile sensation from specific spots in the skin. Brodmann area number 52 represents parainsular region where the temporal lobe and insula meet. The visual cortex is known as Brodmann Area number 17. Area number 10 is the frontmost piece of prefrontal cortex which has increased most in size over the course of evolution and seems to allow us in multitask.

No region of the brain has been as precisely mapped as the somatosensory cortex. This strip of cortex runs roughly over the top of the brain from ear to ear. The left somatosensory cortex receives signal from the right and vice versa. Each part of the body is assigned a particular spot in the somatosensory cortex for processing. As a result, the somatosensory cortex is essentially a map of the body – one that would give Google mappers a heart attack. In experiments in the 1960s, Canadian neurosurgeon Wilder Penfield stimulated systematically different spots of somatosensory cortex and participants reported sensation in different parts of the body. In this way, Penfield was able to "map" the somatosensory cortex, assigning each spot a corresponding part of the body.

There is an element of humour in cortical representation. Although the hand is below the arm, the somatosensory's hand abuts the region that receives signal from the face. Similarly, the somatosensory representation of the genitals lies directly below the feet. It is observed that with more cortical space, a body part becomes more sensitive. The tip of our tongue, which has a larger representation can feel the ridges of our teeth, whereas the back of our hands have smaller somatosensory representation.

Because of the past works, the belief was strengthened and carried forward into the idea that particular patterns of activity must also be hardwired and if not strictly unchangeable, at least persistent. According to this view, mental illness such as depression might be caused by underactivity in some areas of the prefrontal cortex and overactivity in the amygdala and the underlying biology is as permanent as your finger-prints.

However, more recently there has been change in the structure-function relationship.

The Silver Spring Experiments

Edward Taub and associated initiated a bold series of experiments on monkeys in the Institute of Behavioural Research, Silver Spring (Maryland, USA). The neural centres representing sensory connection to fingers were served in monkeys. Animals lost all sensation in those limbs.

The case launched the animal's rights movement in the USA. After the monkey, were rescued and spared any further research. Taub had to face criminal investigation, though he argued that his work was meant for human welfare.

However, the result of these sensory deprivation studies in 1991 was stunning in the field of science that was still stuck in hardwired land. The region of the monkey's somatosensory cortex which originally processed sensations from the fingers, hands and arms had changed jobs. As a result of receiving no signals from the body parts for year after silent year, the region now processed signals from the face instead. Every bit of neuroscience wisdom said that a differentiated region of the brain would simply do the function for which it is hardwired. Yet that was not what happened. The amount of brain now receiving sensations from the face had grown to fourteen square millimeters – a "massive cortical reorganization".

Around the same time, other studies of monkeys showed that adult primate brain can change in response to something much less extreme than amputation or nerve-cutting strategy. In the seminal study, scientists at the University of California, San Francisco trained owl monkeys to develop an acute sense of touch in their fingers. They were trained to brush a spinning disk. Day in and day out, monkeys underwent this exercise, until they had done it hundreds of times. The region of their brain – specifically in somatosensory cortex – that received signals from the finger had been trained to feel the grooves in the spinning disks. Structure-function relationships are not hardwired. Instead, the physical lay-out of the brain – how much space it assigns to which tasks and body parts – is shaped by how an organism behaves.

Just as the region of the brain responsible for feeling the sense of touch in a particular part of the body could change in response to experience, so could the region of the brain responsible for moving a part of the body. When scientists also at UCSF trained monkeys to tap a food pellet with sufficient dexterity to get it out of a tiny cup (one too small to accommodate more than a single monkey finger) they found similar changes in their brains. The region of the motor cortex responsible for moving fingers had doubled, taking over space that had previously controlled other parts of the body.

And what about human experiences? The place to look into the application of findings obtained from animal research involved the study of sensory experiences from those who are blind or deaf.

Seeing the Thunder, Hearing the Lightening
The fine structure of the somatosensory cortex and motor cortex – with the difference between a region the feels or moves a finger and a region that feels or moves a

cheek measured in millimeters – can change in response to experience and behaviour. But the brain is capable of even greater reorganization. Studies of blind and deaf examined much bigger chunks of neural real estate: the visual cortex which occupies nearly one-third of the brain's volume. It is nestled towards the back and the auditory cortex, which stretches across the top of the brain across the ears. We are familiar with a folk wisdom that the blind has especially sharp hearing and the deaf have especially sharp eye sight. But this folk wisdom is not cent percent true. In fact, blind people do not hear softer sounds, and deaf people cannot detect minimal contrasts or see in dimmer light than hearing people can. But compensation works in another way.

In people who are deaf from birth, objects in the peripheral vision are perceived not only in the visual cortex but also in the auditory cortex. **The auditory cortex sees.** It is as if the auditory cortex, tired of enforced inactivity as a result of receiving no signals from the ears, take upon itself a regimen of job retraining, so that it now processes visual signals. This has practical consequences. Deaf people are faster and more accurate at detecting the movement of objects in their peripheral vision than are hearing people.

Something comparable happens in people who are blind from birth or an early age. In them, no signals reach the visual cortex. However, the visual cortex does not go waste. In blind people who become proficient in reading Braille, the visual cortex switches jobs to processing tactile signal from those reading fingers. This discovery was so unexpected that some of neuroscience's most eminent practitioners refused to believe it. As a consequence, the submission turned down by *Science* was published by its arch competitor *Nature* (April 1996).

The brains of the blind change in another way too. When they use their peripheral hearing – to locate the source of a sound, for instance, something they tend to be better at than sighted people – they use their visual cortex. Their brains have undergone what we call compensatory reorganization. As a result, the **visual cortex hears.** Once again William James proved prescient. A century before these discoveries, in his 1892 book *Psychology: The Briefer Course,* he wondered whether if neurons get crossed inside the brain, *"we should hear the lightening and see the thunder"* – a foreshadowing of the profound functional alternations in the brain's primary sensory cortices that can result from experience.

One final example of how extensive brain rewiring can be Blind people use their visual cortex to remember words. Verbal memory is not even a primary sensory ability, yet when the visual cortex is not called on to perform its intended function, it can switch even to this higher-order cognitive function. There is no such activation of the visual region when sighted people recall words. In the blind, the visual cortex also generates verbs in response to nouns (like *throw* for *ball*). Again, it does not perform this function in sighted people. The ability of the visual cortex to process language came as a shock to neuroscientists.

In brief, the brain can change assigning a new function to a region that originally did something else. These conclusions were essentially derived from studies conducted on the blind and the deaf. However, critics argued that what happen to the blind and the deaf may not apply to normal population. This prompted some experimental studies on normal population.

Pascual-Leone and associates conducted experiments involving "virtual piano player". They discovered that merely thinking about players keyboard exercise expanded the region of motor cortex devoted to moving fingers. In another bold experiment, Pascual-Leone recruited a group of healthy volunteers to spend five days in a safe experiment at Beth Israel Deaconess Medical Center in Boston. The participants were blindfolded. To keep from dying of boredom they were provided with sensorially intense activities learning braille and finetuning their hearing. Prior to experimental intervention, they were subjected to fMRI scans. At the end of the five days of such exercise, they were subjected to scans. When they heard something the activity in their visual cortex increased. The visual cortex is supposed to handle sight. Yet, after a mere five days of an unusual sensory activity, scans indicated a radical change in function.

If the visual cortex, which seems like the most hardwired of all the brain's hardwired regions, can so quickly alter its function as a result of sensory input and sensory deprivation, surely it is time to question whether much about to brain really is fixed and unchangeable. In all likelihood the visual cortex did not grow new connections to the ears and fingers, five days wasn't time enough for that. Pascual-Leone suspects that instead "some rudimentary somatosensory and auditory connections to the visual cortex must already be present", left over from the period of brain development when neurons from the eyes and ears and fingers connect to many regions of the cortex rather than just the ones they're supposed to. When input from the retina to the visual cortex ceased because of the blind - fold, the other sensory connections were unmasked. Even neural cables that receive no traffic for decades can start carrying signals again.

Neuroplasticity in the Clinic

The realization that sensory experiences can rewire the brain has had important real-world consequences. The raid on the Silver Spring monkeys cost Edward Taub years of his life as he fought civil and criminal changes, but eventually he returned to research. By the 1990's he had made good on his promise, tapping the power of neuroplasticity discovered in the Silver Spring monkeys – whose brain regions had to be remapped to handle new jobs – to devise a therapy that helped countless stroke patients function again. From the discovery that a region of the monkeys' brains could be retrained to perform a new function, Taub inferred that people in whom a stroke had damaged one region of the brain could train a healthy region of their brain to assume the function of the damaged part.

He called the treatment **constraint-induced movement therapy.** This could be explained with the example in whom a stroke has disabled a region of the motor cortex, leaving one arm paralyzed. Taub would put this patient good arm in a sling and her good hand in an oven mitt for about 90 percent of waking hours for about fourteen straight days, so she could not use either, leaving her no choice but to try to use her paralyzed arm in the activities of daily living and the rehabilitation exercise he advised. These exercises, six hours a day for two five-day weeks, involved intensive use of the "paralyzed" arm – which was actually slightly functional. The patient manipulated cups and eating utensils, played cards and picked up sandwiches. After scores of hours of practice, most patients made huge improvements and this improvement occurred not just in recent stroke patients, but even in those who had suffered strokes years before.

They gained their ability to brush their teeth, comb their hair, drink from a glass and the like.

Brain imaging revealed the reason for this success. Taub found what he called "a large use-dependent brain reorganization in which substantial new areas of the brain are recruited" to take over the function of region that has been disabled by stroke. The area responsible for producing movements of the affected arm almost doubles in size, and parts of the brain that are not normally involved, areas adjacent, are recruited. This is the first time an experiment had demonstrated the rewiring of the brain as a result of physical therapy after a stroke.

Brain plasticity may take several forms: (a) In some patients, an adjacent region in the motor cortex assume the function of the disabled region. (b) In others, the premotor cortex, which usually plans movements and does not order them executed, take over for the damaged region of the motor cortex. (c) And in other patients, the brain reorganization is truly dramatic. If the stroke has disabled the right motor cortex (leaving the left arm paralyzed), then the corresponding region of the left motor cortex takes over, yet with no apparent effect on the ability to do its original job of moving the right arm. In short, the brain has the power to recruit healthy neurons to perform the function of the damaged one. Neuroplasticity enables the brain to reassign jobs.

Despite such spectacular achievements, there were critics who argued that the findings are limited only to stroke patients. Taub recruited violinists and other string musicians for brain-imaging study. He examined the regions that control four fingers. Taub discovered that his musicians were not different from monkeys. In the violinists, the amount of space in the somatosensory cortex devoted to registering feeling from the digits of the left hand was much greater than in the nonmusicians, especially in those who began playing seriously before age twelve. Brain exposed to the demands of playing the violin undergo extensive alternations, displaying use-dependent cortical reorganization.

Plasticity is an intrinsic property of the human brain. The potential of the adult brain to reprogram itself might be much greater than has previously been assumed (Pascual-Leone, 2005). Neuroplasticity allows the brain to break the bonds of its own genome, which dictate that one region will "see" and another will "hear". The genetical guided blueprint is fine for most people under most conditions, but not all of us all the time – not when we lose our sight or suffer a stroke. **The brain is neither immutable nor static, but continuously remodeled by the lives we lead.**

Mind over Matter

It is important to recollect the experiment in which mere thinking about performing a piano exercise expands the region of the motor cortex responsible for moving those fingers. Two other brilliant experiments also demonstrate that mind changes the brain.

1.   Neuro psychiatrist, Jeffrey Schwartz (UCLA) was treating OCD patients. Brain imaging showed hyperactivity in two areas. Orbital frontal cortex (whose main job is to notice if something is amiss) and the striatum (which receives input from orbital frontal cortex and the amygdala). These two regions together are called the *worry circuit.* Although antidepressants including Prozac, Paxil, and Zoloft help somewhat, Schwartz found that Buddhist meditation practice, called *mindfulness* or mindful awareness provided relatively stable solutions.

The methods involve attending just to the bare facts of perception as presented either through the five physical senses or through mind without reacting to them by deed, speech or by mental comments. The neuroimaging showed dramatic fall in the activity of the worry circuit. **Thinking about inner thought in a new way alters patterns of brain activity.**

2.   Cognitive behaviour therapy is a form of mental training. The idea is reappraise dysfunctional thinking, helping people escape the pattern in which they are imprisoned.

In short, the revolution in neuroplasticity has shown that the brain can change as a result of the distinct inputs. It can change as a result of the experience we have in the world – how we move and behave and what sensory signals arrive in our cortex. The brain can change in response to purely mental activity, ranging from meditation to cognitive-behaviour therapy, with the result that activity in specific circuits can increase or decrease.

Chapter 16

Neuroscience of
Transformational Leadership

(Source: Based on the research article "Differentiating transformational and non-transformational leaders on the basis of neurological imaging" published in The Leadership Quarterly, 2012, 23 pp. 244-258)

The construct of transformational leadership developed as a reaction to the inadequacy in the mainstream leadership research. One HBR article pointed out that managers are not truly leaders since managers mostly do the maintenance functions while leaders bring about attitudinal and behavioural transformations in followers. Thus, a distinction was made between *transactional (maintenance) leaders and transformational leaders.* Around the same time, there was a big happening in Chrysler Automobile company in the U.S. A person by the name Lee Iacocca took over as the G.M. of the company and he made several drastic changes. The changes were transformational in nature. The success was miraculous and people spoke of Iacocca syndrome. Because of these events, research was directed towards the issue of transformational leadership/charismatic leadership.

Charisma is not a new word, but it was mostly restricted to sectors of politics and religion. It was for the first time people realized the possibility of charismatic leadership in organizations.

It is important to recognize that the expressions such as transformational, charismatic, visionary and authentic leaderships are used interchangeably. All these expressions are similar and they can be placed under the common rubric *inspirational leadership*. However, there is some difference across the terms. The word transformational emphasizes the process of change whereas charisma stresses the process of impact of leaders. In contrast, the expression visionary emphasizes mentage image of the leaders and authentic aspect puts stress on ethical consideration. In sum, all these terms imply new look approach to leadership and these all forms of *inspirational leadership*.

Let us go beyond the terms and identify features of TL.

Parameters of TL

R.N. Kanungo, a prominent researcher in the field of charismatic leadership has identified five dimensions: sensitivity to environmental gaps, sensitivity to members' needs, vision, articulation, and uniqueness of strategy. Kanungo has developed a psychometric measure for charismatic leadership.

Another psychometric measure that has been used in the literature involves Multifactor Leadership Questionnaire (MLQ) developed by Bass. The scale contains four items for each of the following dimensions: inspirational motivation, idealized influence, intellectual stimulation, individualized consideration, and attributed charisma.

The Study

Balthazard, Waldman, Thatcher and Hannah (2012) report a study of neurological indicators of TL were identified.

The Procedure

In the beginning a sample of 200 individuals (135 business and community leaders, 33 mid-career Army officers and 32 officers in military academy) was listed for study. In a face-to-face session, a set of 19 electrodes to the scalp of participants was fastened and the EEG activity was assessed.

The basic objectives of the statistical method of analysis involved discriminant analysis. The discriminant analysis is helpful to find out the specific neurological activities (out of all possible dependent measures of EEG activities) that correctly distinguish TL leaders from non-TL leaders. It may be indicated that TL and non-TL leaders were initially categorized on the basis of psychometric method of MLQ.

Findings

The application of discriminant analysis (a multivariate statistical tool) to identify neurological indicators of TL leaders as opposed to non-TL leaders showed three important findings.

First, it was shown that there is greater activity in the pre-frontal cortex in TL leaders. This is an obvious expectation from TL leaders since prefrontal activity is linked with planning, decision making and self-control. It is important to recognize that a greater self-control helps TL leaders for emotional regulation and emotional management.

Second, next to higher prefrontal activity, activities in *temporal lobe* are predominant in TL leaders. This is so because the temporal lobes play critical role in memory, perception, language and personality. The hippocampal system located in this region is important for forming a coherent set of memories of people and events. This is helpful in understanding engagement in the present. The temporal lobes also mediate the balance between one's psychological state and transaction with others and the environment. As TL leaders require adept social perception (e.g. individualized consideration) and reasoning skills, the functions of temporal lobes are critical for TL leaders.

Third, hemispheric differences are identified. A greater degree of right brain activity is noticed among TL leaders. The plausible reasons include a number of considerations. An increased level of integration or *holistic processing* within the right hemisphere is an asset for TL leaders. It contributes to emotional balance through integration in the processes that manage emotional thought. Emotional control of one-self and the understanding of emotional reactions on the part of others may be relevant to TL leaders. It has been shown that dysfunction in the right frontal portion of the brain results in an inability to understand relationships with others. The right hemisphere of the brain is key to understanding how leaders form a understanding of *bigger picture*.

In conclusion, the empirical study has demonstrated that TL leaders can be distinguished from non-TL leaders on the basis of a validated discriminant function derived from EEG data. Research of this nature can provide insights as to the neurological origins of the form of leadership.

Selected References

Bossons, R., Riddell, P. & Sartain, D. (2025). *The neuroscience of leadership coaching*. London: Bloomsbury

Davidson, R. & Begley, S. (2012). *The emotional life of your brain*. New York: Hudson Street Press.

Ekman, P. (2007). *Emotions revisted*. New York: Owl Books

Fiori, N. (2006). *Cognitive neuroscience*. New Delhi: Prentice Hall of India.

Goldberg, E. (2009). *The new executive brain*. New York: Oxford University Press.

Goleman, D. (1996). *Emotional intelligence*. London: Bloomsbury.

Kahneman, D. (2012). *Thinking fast and slow*. Penguin

BLACK EAGLE BOOKS

www.blackeaglebooks.org
info@blackeaglebooks.org

Black Eagle Books, an independent publisher, was founded as a nonprofit organization in April, 2019. It is our mission to connect and engage the Indian diaspora and the world at large with the best of works of world literature published on a collaborative platform, with special emphasis on foregrounding Contemporary Classics and New Writing.

www.ingramcontent.com/pod-product-compliance
Lightning Source LLC
Chambersburg PA
CBHW020543030426
42337CB00013B/957